nibble munch chomp

The art and science of feeding your pet

Published by JoJo Publishing in conjunction with Lort Smith Animal Hospital

nibble munch chomp
The art and science of feeding your pet

Published by JoJo Publishing
'Yarra's Edge'
2203/80 Lorimer Street
Docklands Vic 3008
Australia
Email: jo-media@bigpond.net.au or visit www.jojopublishing.com

In conjunction with

Lort Smith Animal Hospital
24 Villiers Street
North Melbourne Vic 3051
Australia
www.lortsmith.com

National Library of Australia Cataloguing-in-Pulication data:
Herbert, Sasha.
Nibble munch chomp: the art and science of feeding your pet.

ISBN 9780980283679 (pbk.).

1. Pets – Feeding and feeds – Recipes. 2. Pets – Nutrition.
I. Title.

636.085

Edited by Jim Howes
Photography by Belinda Russo
Designed by The Modern Art Production Group
Typeset by The Modern Art Production Group
Printed in China by Everbest Printing

Lort Smith Animal Hospital

nibble munch chomp

The art and science of feeding your pet

Dr Sasha Herbert Senior Vet at the Lort Smith Animal Hospital

Photography by Belinda Russo Animal Management Officer

Foreword

For many years I have spent a great deal of my time trying to stimulate people's ideas about food and cooking. I have tried to pass on my enthusiasm for how cooking for friends and family can be a wonderful experience – both for the cook and those who eat the meal. Eating is a social event, something that brings us together. Discovering new ways to feed our families and friends is a constant and hugely satisfying adventure. My philosophy is give it a go. Try that new recipe. Enjoy your attempts. You are probably a much better cook than you thought you were and, if not, don't be disheartened. You soon will be.

Until now, I have always been thinking of people in my work. Sasha's new book changes that.

Here are more than 100 recipes for meals for dogs, cats, birds, lizards, rabbits and guinea pigs and various other pets. There are staple foods and special treats, handy snacks and nibbles for when you take your pet out. Sasha's recipes are simple and effective and are often suitable for more than one species – some of the recipes we can eat too. But the intention is the same as with any good cook book. It's about learning how to please those special to us and it's about sharing the great experience of eating together. Jump into this book. Devour it. Your 'best mates' will thank you for the effort a thousand times over.

Gabriel Gaté
Celebrity chef and cookery author

Contents

Introduction	ix
The art and science of feeding your pet	x
The key	xi
The Lort Smith Animal Hospital	xii
Dogs	1
Cats	73
Ferrets	107
Birds	125
Reptiles	151
Rabbits and guinea pigs	173
Rodents	189
Glossary	199
Index	200

Dry food meatballs (page 54)

Introduction

People have centuries of emotional myth and magic associated with food and the art of feeding. We have comfort food and healing tonics. The Chinese consider different ingredients to be heating and cooling. We have refreshing and revitalising drinks, mood-lifting desserts and nostalgic dinners, relaxing cups of tea and invigorating sorbets. A meal can be relaxed or formal, and there are different manners to go with each, wherever you are from.

As humans, planning what we are going to eat and how we will eat it forms an integral part of our emotional lives. It is rarely a function we perform just to keep us alive, like breathing! Feeding is an integral part of nurturing our relationships, not least with our animals.

We keep pets because we are social creatures. Even when using a fully balanced kibble diet, there is so much more you can put into feeding your animal. Feeding an animal well requires an owner to use the balanced commercial diets available or to learn about and formulate a balanced diet prepared at home. No matter which method you use, it is important to feed with passion and dedication.

I've come to the conclusion that, after science, art is necessary to produce and modify a diet appropriate to an animal's needs in a particular situation. You must be flexible, observant and objective in your responses to your animal's demands, while avoiding being trained by the animal. At the same time, love is a very important ingredient.

As a new graduate vet, I treated many farm animals that had become sick because of dietary deficiencies, toxicities and imbalances in their diets. Ostrich chicks developed twisted legs due to poor vitamin balance. Emus laid soft-shelled eggs because the mineral balance in their food wasn't quite right. Dogs and dairy cows ran out of calcium when they started to lactate. Beef cows and guinea pigs ran out of energy because their pregnancies drained more energy than expected from their food intake.

Problems varied with the season and with the age and sex of the animals involved. They also varied with the types of management of the animals. The farmers would employ our services to treat the animals after they had become sick. They would then have to try to find a way to prevent the animals getting sick. This started to intrigue me. Why was it that the same diet could be fed to a two separate flocks of ostriches and it worked for one and not the other? This is something I developed a much better feel for as my work took me from farms, zoos, wildlife sanctuaries and rescue centres, and finally back to companion animals.

This book contains a collection of recipes and stories from the staff at the Lort Smith Animal Hospital and from my veterinary adventures elsewhere. I have covered most of the pets we see commonly in veterinary practice in urban Australia, and there will be many more that aren't mentioned. No matter what species your pet is, I would like to encourage all pet owners to educate themselves about what their pet needs. There is plenty of information out there in libraries, vet clinics, clubs and societies, and the internet. Your pet depends on you so take responsibility for what you are doing. Feed from the heart but keep on learning. Be interested in discovering new possibilities. Swap recipes with friends. Take care but be inventive. Enjoy yourself!

Sasha Herbert – Senior Vet – Lort Smith Animal Hospital

The art and science of feeding your pet

Omnivore. Carnivore. Herbivore. Frugivore. Granivore. Nectarivore. Piscivore. Folivore. Insectivore. What heading does your pet come under? There are some great words for the things that animals eat. Although most of our pets are vertebrates, they have completely different digestive systems. Dogs, cats and ferrets are all carnivores (although, in the 'Dogs' chapter, you will see that they are really omnivores) and yet they need different diets. Australian freshwater turtles are also carnivores but they don't like dog food very much! Snakes are carnivores but their prey is different from that of a tiger. Budgies and cockatoos are granivores, meaning they eat mostly grains and seeds, but the birds are of very different sizes and capabilities. Rainbow lorikeets are nectarivores: they eat nectar. Penguins are piscivores and eat fish. Langurs, a group of stunning Asian monkeys, are folivores and eat leaves. Echidnas are insectivores and we all know what they eat.

These terms are a useful general guide but can also be a little misleading if taken too literally. Carnivores do indeed eat a meat-based diet. It is easy to assume that this means they eat only the skeletal muscle of animals. We tend to think of meat as beef, pork, bacon, fish, chicken and so on. However, the term 'carnivore' refers to animals who eat other animals, and they don't just stick to the muscle meat. If they did, they would be lacking all sorts of important minerals, vitamins, fibre and fats.

The basic nutritional requirements of an animal are often expressed in percentages of protein, fat, carbohydrate and fibre. If the animal is well-studied, vitamin and mineral requirements are also available. A diet is developed to meet these requirements. It consists of a list of ingredients and amounts of ingredients. There are a huge number of possible combinations of ingredients, ways of preparing them and of offering them. This is where the joy and problems of feeding begin. Feeding practices are based on a combination of science, tradition, labour resources, skills and equipment available. They can vary according to the climate, season and what the animals are required to do. Lifestyle, behaviour and size can also create needs for different types and amounts of nutrients.

Water is essential for life. It is the most important nutrient in your pet's diet and should not be underestimated. No matter what the species, all animals require water to survive. None of the other ingredients will be of any use to the body if there is no water to complement them. Interesting differences between species' water requirements become apparent when you look at the lifestyles of wild animals. It's easy to see where a wolf or a tiger would get its water from. They live in places where water is relatively plentiful in rivers, lakes, and even puddles. Where does a koala get its water? How does a python drink? Where do desert-dwelling lizards find water? They all need it. Even the mythically drought-tolerant camel needs it. In the following chapters, I'll give you some ideas on how to provide water for your pets in an appropriate way.

Finally, it is very important to check what might be toxic to your animal as many foods that we can eat safely are toxic to certain other species. On the other hand, certain animals can eat things that would make us terribly ill. I'll discuss foods to be avoided and the dangers involved at the end of each chapter.

I won't take you through the science of developing a well-balanced diet for your pet. That information can be found elsewhere. What I hope to do is to give you some ideas on how to cook at home for your pet. I really hope that you will read the stories about different species of pets and not just about those you own. All of these animals are fascinating and beautiful, and you can find all sorts of new ideas when you look in unusual places.

This book is all about creating a simple work of love for those that you love. I hope that it inspires you to learn more about your pet's needs and to create meals with knowledge and passion. Food is the way to your pet's heart!

The key

Matching recipes to pets:
Many of the recipes described in this book can be used for several different species. You will find 'suitable for' above each recipe, indicating which pets the recipes can be offered to.

The possibilities are:

- human
- dog
- cat
- ferret
- bird
- lizard
- turtle
- rabbit
- guinea pig
- rodent

Please refer to the appropriate chapter for your pet for more detail on what can be offered to each species.

Preparation times:
You will find 'preparation time' above each recipe, indicating roughly how long it will take to prepare and cook. The possible categories are:

Short: 5–15 mins to prepare and cook
Medium: 15–45 mins
Long: over 45 mins to prepare and cook overnight

The Lort Smith Animal Hospital

The Lort Smith Animal Hospital has provided quality care to millions of animals over its 78-year history. Its vision is a world in which animals are respected and where the bond between people and animals is understood and valued.

Based in Melbourne, Australia, it was founded by Mrs Lort Smith who had a passion for lost, abandoned, mistreated, sick and injured animals. It is now the largest animal hospital in the southern hemisphere, with a staff of over 150, and a volunteer workforce exceeding 500. Together they tend to the needs of more than 100,000 animals a year.

The hospital is a non-profit organisation which receives no government funding. It continues to provide care for animals belonging to people of limited means, promotes responsible pet ownership and fosters an awareness of animals and the benefits they bring.

Proceeds from the sales of this book and other related publications will help in this important work.

PLEASE HELP US HELP ANIMALS AT RISK — a donation will support this vital work and make an enormous contribution to the welfare of the thousands of animals at risk.

ALL DONATIONS OVER $2 ARE NOW FULLY TAX DEDUCTIBLE

Donations can be made at www.lortsmith.com

dogs

what do dogs need?

4
Meals

26
Beverages

29
Party food, treats and snacks

48
Food as entertainment

52
Dogs feeling poorly

70
Food that dogs should avoid

Dogs need love, entertainment, security, shelter and devotion. They need a family willing to care for them in sickness and in health. We are responsible for their every need and therefore we must seek out the knowledge needed to provide the best care for them. It's the natural thing to do but often it's the last.

Dogs. Are they carnivores? Are they really like wolves, hyenas and jackals? Or are they more like us? Is it foolish to feed them only meat? Should they be fed what their human family eats? The truth encompasses a little of each.

In the wild, other hunting animals that seem similar to dogs, such as wolves and hyenas, eat fruit, leaves, grasses, dig for roots and even obtain vegetable matter from the stomachs of their prey. The bones of their prey provide calcium and help keep their teeth clean. Their diets are highly varied and also change seasonally.

A domestic dog fed on a human diet struggles with dairy products and can actually be poisoned by some of the common ingredients in human pantries. (See page 70 on what not to feed your dog.) The pitfalls of feeding a home-cooked diet are that it is very hard to balance and very easy to overlook the ways in which it isn't balanced until the dog becomes ill. However, this does not mean it can't be done. With a little research and attention to detail, dogs can do very well on a diet of home cooking.

That's enough! The science of nutrition can be found elsewhere. This book is about eating together and experimenting with new ingredients. It's about outings and special occasions, Friday night takeaway with your best canine friend, a warm cup of soup together on a winter's day, rewards for obeying commands, puzzles to entertain him while you're out, soothing recipes to support her when she's sick and,of course, party food!

Bacon and cheese dog biscuits (page 40)

Meals

Dogs are actually omnivorous. They need a lot less meat protein than cats, ferrets or snakes, and feeding a high animal protein diet to a dog will take a toll on its health. A dog is designed to digest a wide range of plant and animal products. Dogs must eat more than just muscle meat. They need plenty of carbohydrates and fibre from vegetable and plant matter and only a very small amount of fat. Their protein can come from both plant and animal products. The other things to consider are sources of minerals such as calcium and phosphorous and of course vitamins.

A dog's dinner

This recipe was a favourite of my beautiful Samoyed, Jasmine. She was a gorgeous white shaggy dog with a big smile. My family adopted her from an animal shelter many years ago. We went to the shelter ostensibly looking for a dog for a friend of the family. Walking along the rows of cages with all those sad eyes or frantically wagging tails is one of the hardest things to do. If only we could take them all home. Jasmine chose us by putting her paw up on the cage door and looking mournfully at my mother under her long lashes as we said hello. That was it. We were hers for life! This is what my mother used to cook for Jasmine.

Jasmine's meatloaf

I have written this recipe using minced beef, rice and any vegies. You can also make it using left over cooked vegies and any chutneys left in the fridge for extra flavour. This is a bulk recipe. After it is cooked it can be stored in individual portions in the freezer.

suitable for

dog, cat, ferret, turtle, lizard

preparation time

Long: over 45 minutes to prepare and cook.

ingredients

1 kg beef mince
2 eggs
1 tablespoon tomato paste
2 cups breadcrumbs
2 cups grated carrot (1 large carrot)
1 cup chopped celery (1 stick including leaves)
2 tablespoons soy sauce
1 large garlic clove (chopped)
1 cup raw rice

method

Preheat oven to 170 °C (150 °C if fan-forced).
Add the rice to a large pot of boiling water. Boil for 15 minutes.
Strain and allow it to cool.
Add all the ingredients, including the rice, to the pot previously used for the rice and stir thoroughly.
Spread evenly about 5 cm thick across a deep oven tray.
Bake for 40 minutes.

serve

Serve cooled portions with canivore gravy (page 35) or relish (no onions).

tip

Fruit and vegetable pulp can be used as an alternative for the celery in this recipe. Use the fresh pulp left over after juicing fruit and vegetables. (See page 54 for liver tonic.)

Jasmine's meatloaf

Dogs, diabetes and diet

Bonnie was a diabetic poodle cross. She did not have enough of her own insulin to control her blood glucose. She was diagnosed when her owner brought her in to the vet because she had been drinking and urinating copiously. Bonnie stayed in hospital while her blood glucose was brought under control and the appropriate dose of insulin was calibrated for her. This involved feeding Bonnie identical meals with identical energy levels twice daily. For most dogs, the easiest way to do this is to feed one of the prescription diets. However, we found that Bonnie just flatly refused to eat these diets as she had been fed home cooked food all her life, she felt sick and she missed her owner. None of the usual enticement methods worked (have a look at page 68 on enrichment for some ideas).

We needed her to eat so that we could calibrate her insulin dose correctly. I asked her owner to tell me the ingredients she usually fed Bonnie at home. These included a mixture of chicken, rice and sometimes vegetables. I offered Bonnie some roast chicken in the hospital and she ate it ravenously. Hooray! We developed a recipe for Bonnie and included those ingredients, some oils, salts and some calcium to balance it out. She went home to her owner two days later and the same recipe was used to feed her at home.

Consistency seems to be the key to dietary support in the treatment of canine diabetes.

Roast chicken and sautéed vegetables

suitable for

dog, lizard, human

preparation time

Medium: 15–45 minutes to prepare and cook.

ingredients

2 whole chickens
1 cup rice
1 carrot finely sliced
4 fine slices of pumpkin
¼ head of broccoli chopped to stir-fry size
olive oil
stock

method

Dry roast the chickens, debone and slice.
Cook the rice by the absorption method in either water or stock.
Sauté the sliced vegetables in a little olive oil.
When cooked slice the chicken.
Mix all ingredients together.

serve

Serve cool.

tip

There is enough here for a week for a 20 kg dog but adjust according to your dog's requirements.
Do not feed your dog cooked bones (see page 71).

Roast chicken and sautéed vegetables

Michela is the devoted owner of Georgia and Lupina, the keeshonds. They are great big fluffy teddy bears of dogs and have been doted on since puppyhood. Michela would often cook for her 'girls' and this was one of their favourite recipes. They would jump around stamping their feet for the roast chicken (page 8). If it was boiled instead they were still happy to eat it but there was no animation. They just sat patiently.

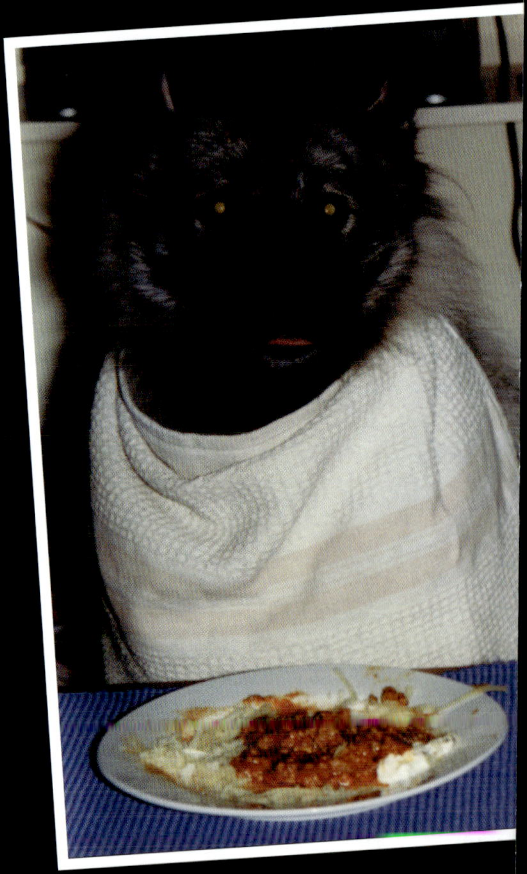

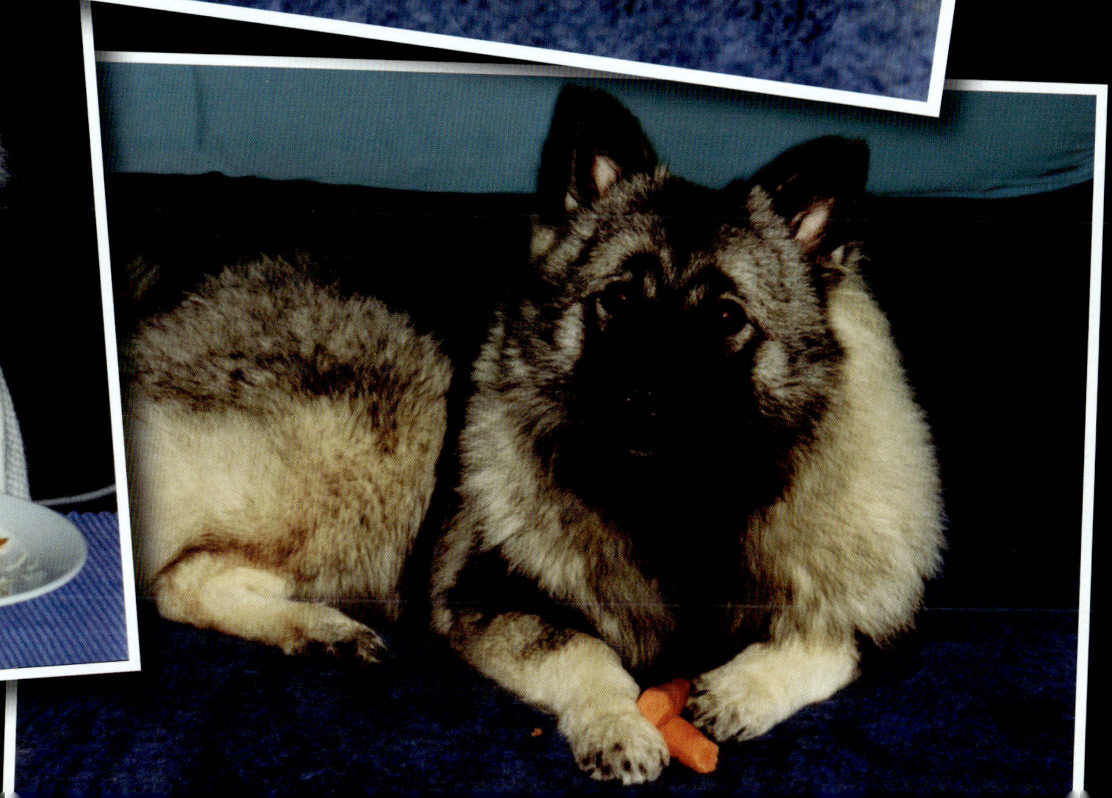

Pork and pear stir-fry

Dogs will love this but most cats prefer it without rice, spinach or bean sprouts.

suitable for

dog, lizard, human

preparation time

Short: 5–15 minutes to prepare and cook.

ingredients

200 g pork, trimmed of fat and finely sliced
1 pear, finely sliced
¼ red capsicum, finely sliced
2 teaspoons vegetable oil

marinade

¼ teaspoon grated ginger
1 teaspoon light soy sauce
¼ teaspoon ground coriander
juice of 1 lime
1 teaspoon sesame oil

method

Mix the marinade by combining the sesame oil, ground coriander, ginger, lime and soy sauce.
Marinate the pork pieces for at least two hours.
Drain the pork pieces reserving the marinade.
Fry the capsicum in some of the vegetable oil until it softens but doesn't lose colour. Remove from the pan.
Add the rest of the oil and the pork to the pan for a couple of minutes then return the capsicum to pan. Add the sliced pears and toss it all together for another minute.
Remove from the pan.
Heat the marinade in the pan until boiling and then remove from the heat.

serve

This dish should be served cool with rice and the marinade poured over it. An alternative is to serve it on a bed of baby spinach leaves or bean sprouts.

Beef casserole

suitable for
dog, cat

preparation time
Medium: 15–45 minutes to prepare and cook.

ingredients
2.5 kg finely chopped beef
¾ cup canola oil
4 garlic cloves, chopped
2 litres water
8 cups grated or blended vegies (carrots, celery, broccoli, cauliflower, bean sprouts, potatoes, sweet potatoes, capsicum, spinach, lettuce, tomatoes — anything from the fridge as long as it's not onion!)
2–3 cans kidney beans
½ cup molasses
4 cups oatmeal
2 eggs

method
Brown the meat with canola oil and garlic in a large casserole pot.
When cooked, add the water, vegies, kidney beans and oatmeal.
Bring to the boil.
Simmer for 10 minutes, stirring constantly while thickening.
Allow to cool and separate into meal-sized portions to be frozen for future use.

Shepherd's pie

suitable for
dog, cat, ferret, human

preparation time
Medium: 15–45 minutes to prepare and cook.

ingredients
250 g cooked minced beef or yesterday's roast beef, lamb or pork (no bones)
2 tablespoons flour
1 teaspoon chopped parsley
¼ teaspoon chopped thyme (or a pinch of the dried version)
¼ teaspoon chopped marjoram (or a pinch of the dried version)
salt and pepper
120 ml beef stock
250 g doggy mashed potatoes
tomato sauce

method
Preheat oven to 180 °C.
Grease a pie dish.
If using yesterday's roast then chop it very finely. (Remember, no bones as they have been cooked).
Add the herbs, flour and tomato sauce, and season with salt and pepper.
Add the stock and stir until boiling.
Line the greased pie dish with a layer of the mashed potatoes.
Pour the meat mixture in.
Spread the remainder of the potato on top.
Smooth and mark with a fork.
Glaze with milk.
Brown and heat for about 30 minutes.

serve
Serve cool.

Mashed potato

suitable for
dog, cat, human

preparation time
Short: 5–15 minutes to prepare and cook.

ingredients
3 potatoes, peeled and cubed
1 tablespoon margarine
1 tablespoon natural yoghurt
¼ cup grated cheese

method
Boil the potatoes until tender. Strain.
Add the margarine and yoghurt to the pan over low heat. Stir until combined.
Turn off the heat.
Return the potatoes to the pan with the yoghurt and margarine. Add the cheese.
Mash the ingredients and mix together well.

serve
Serve cool.

Friday night takeaway

Frank, the Irish water spaniel, greeted his tired owner who arrived home exhausted after an extra long meeting at work. There was no dog food left in the cupboard and no enthusiasm left for a walk. Frank, however, had spent the day quietly sniffing around the garden and occasionally running enthusiastically to the gate when he heard the neighbour's cockatoo calling his name. Frank had no idea that cockatoos could be so good at mimicry. When his owner finally arrived he was desperately excited, dying for a walk and absolutely starving. He leapt upon his owner lavishing him with affection and all he received in response was a desultory pat and a command of 'get down Frank'. His owner saw the dejection in Frank's tail and realised what they both needed was an outing and an easy dinner in the park. What could they both have? Kebabs! Frank would have his without garnishing sauces but definitely with lettuce and flat bread. His owner wouldn't have to cook for them both or wait until after taking the dog for a walk to have dinner. Frank could go for his walk around the park and have a special dinner with his owner. A perfect Friday takeaway!

Osso bucco

Osso bucco is great on a cold winter's afternoon when you feel like cooking something slowly.
Cats love the marrow from the veal shanks. Dogs just love the entire dish. If humans are sharing, make two batches and add some wine and onions to the human version.

suitable for

dog, ferret, human

preparation time

Long: over 45 minutes to prepare and cook.

ingredients

500 g veal knuckles
plain flour
½ carrot, sliced
1 tin tomatoes, broken up
½ stick celery, sliced
1 clove garlic, crushed
1 tablespoon olive oil
1 strip lemon rind
200 ml chicken or beef stock
basil and oregano leaves

method

Simmer carrot, celery and garlic in a little of the olive oil.
Dust the veal shanks in flour. Remove vegetables from the pot.
Brown the veal in the remaining oil.
Add the vegies, lemon rind, stock and tomatoes plus a few herb leaves.
Cook for two and a half hours at 160 °C (or 140 °C in a fan-forced oven).

serve

Serve cool with doggy mashed potato (page 13) or rice.

caution

Remove bones before serving as cooked bones are dangerous to your dog. Scrape the marrow out and mix it into the osso bucco as it adds flavour.

Osso bucco

Can your dog be vegetarian?

There are so many recipes with meat. What about the vegetarian dogs? That inspires an interesting debate. As we discussed earlier, dogs are not strictly carnivores. It is possible for them to get all the nutrients they need from a diet made up entirely of ingredients of plant origin. However, that is an extremely difficult diet to balance at home and I have seen several dogs become very sick on improperly balanced vegetarian diets due to malnourishment. I have also met a few very healthy happy dogs that are fed vegetarian diets. I don't advise vegetarian diets for dogs but this doesn't mean that they will become ill if they miss out on meat every now and then. In fact, they love many recipes that are free of animal products, despite their sharp canine teeth!

Lentil pasties

suitable for
dog

preparation time
Long: 45 minutes to prepare and cook.

ingredients
1 packet frozen puff pastry
1 cup brown lentils, soaked overnight
1 cup split peas, soaked overnight.
1 cup red lentils
1 sweet potato, cubed
1 stick celery, sliced
2 cloves garlic, finely chopped
1 teaspoon cumin
1 teaspoon grated ginger
1 teaspoon turmeric
3 cups vegetable stock
1 tablespoon olive oil

method
Stir-fry the garlic and celery in a little olive oil over moderate heat.
Add the stock, all the lentils and split peas, potato and spices.
Bring to the boil, then simmer to reduce while stirring frequently (35 mins).
Preheat the oven to 230 °C.
Grease a flat baking tray.
Lay sheets of puff pastry on a cutting board.
Divide lentil mix across the pastry.
Top with another piece of pastry and press the pastry together between portions.
Use a bread knife to divide your pasties.
Baste each with milk.
Bake for 20 minutes or until golden brown.

serve
Serve when cool.

Beef and spinach stir-fry

suitable for
dog, cat, lizard

preparation time
Short: 5–15 minutes to prepare and cook.

ingredients
300 g beef strips
½ cup chopped spinach
25 g ground raw beef liver
½ tablespoon olive oil
¼ teaspoon grated ginger
1½ cups boiled or steamed white rice

method
Cook the rice first. You only need one and a half cups of cooked rice.
Add oil, ginger, ground liver and beef to a frying pan on medium heat. Stir frequently while cooking until beef is cooked through.
Turn heat off and add cooked rice and chopped spinach.

serve
Serve when cool.

tips
If your dog likes more gravy then add 2 tablespoons of water when the beef is almost cooked.
Flax seed oil is an excellent source of omega fatty acids for dogs but it doesn't smell great. Try using it in this recipe instead of olive oil if your vet has suggested your dog's diet needs supplementing.

Vegetable and beef risotto

suitable for
dog, human

preparation time
Long: over 45 minutes to prepare and cook.

ingredients
1 carrot, cut into long slices about 0.5 cm thick
1 zucchini, sliced about 0.5 cm thick
4 slices pumpkin, cut into slices the same dimensions as the carrot
1 tablespoon olive oil
1 crushed garlic clove
1 cup of rice
beef stock
fresh parsley

method
Preheat oven to 140 °C
Dry roast the vegetable strips until soft and sweet (about 1 hour).
Add the olive oil and crushed garlic to a pan and stir the uncooked rice into it over medium heat.
Heat the beef stock to boiling then bring back to a simmer.
Use the stock to cook the rice by absorption method.
Cut the roasted vegetables into 2 cm strips.
Mix the rice, vegetables and parsley together.

serve
Serve when cooled.

Lentil pasties

Querelle

Pets are our special companions. We like to have dinner and break bread with family and friends. It's all part of the bonding process for both humans and animals. Although there are rules about not feeding pets at the table and feeding strategies to maintain appropriate hierarchies in pack situations, it is still very much part of our nature to want to share food with our pets. It is interesting speaking to vets, vet nurses and support staff who spend their lives with animals. When I ask them what sort of special treats or meals they prepare for their animals many of them say they only feed commercial pet food. It is only when I delve deeper and give examples of my own that I get some very interesting and often delightful answers.

One of the vets I work with has a little Staffordshire bull terrier cross named Querelle. She likes to share her meals with her pets sometimes. She discovered by accident that he is very fond of chilli spiced dishes when he vacuumed up half of her takeaway vindaloo one evening. Now she cooks up a special treat for him and adds soy sauce and chilli to it. She assured me there were no untidy or uncomfortable consequences the next day. Here is a variation on her recipe.

Chilli soy kangaroo

suitable for

dog

preparation time

Short: 5–15 minutes to prepare and cook.

ingredients

- 200 g kangaroo pet mince or strips
- 1 teaspoon chilli sauce
- 1 tablespoon soy sauce
- 1 bok choy, chopped coarsely (or finely if your dog avoids vegetables)
- 1 medium sized carrot, finely sliced
- 1 tablespoon of sunflower oil

method

Stir-fry the kangaroo and carrots in the oil until the kangaroo is cooked through. If you use the sesame seeds add them at the start while heating the oil so that they're crunchy.

Add the soy sauce (and a tablespoon of water if the carrots are still too firm for your dog's preference) while still on the heat. Stir the bok choy and chilli sauce through and take it off the heat.

serve

Serve when cooled.

Canine couscous

suitable for

dog, cat, ferret, human

preparation time

Short: 5–15 minutes to prepare and cook.

ingredients

- ½ cup couscous
- ½ cup boiled water
- 1 teaspoon margarine
- 1 piece bacon, sliced
- ¼ cup fresh flat leafed parsley, chopped
- 1 pinch cumin

method

Pour the boiling water over the couscous in a bowl. Add the margarine and stir quickly with a fork. Cover and allow to sit.

Stir-fry the bacon with the cumin until the bacon is crispy.

Add the bacon and parsley to the couscous. Mix well.

Canine couscous

Beef and pork bolognese

This is a great way to get a fussy feeder to eat some vegetables and to use some of your leftovers. If the vegies are already cooked it only takes a few minutes.

suitable for

dog, cat, ferret

preparation time

Medium: 15–45 minutes to prepare and cook.

ingredients

200 g lean mince beef
100 g minced pork
1 tablespoon olive oil
¼ cup pureed steamed carrot
¼ cup pureed steamed cauliflower
¼ cup pureed steamed celery
2 tablespoons tomato paste

method

Steam the vegetables.
Stir-fry both the beef and pork mince in the olive oil until golden brown.
Vegetables can be puréed by pushing them through a sieve.
Add the puréed vegetables and tomato paste to the mince.

serve

Serve with rice, pasta or even in a toasted sandwich once cooled.

Bone cruncher

This is a meal fit for a (lion) king. Cats and dogs love to eat raw bones if they are introduced to them as kittens or puppies. They are the perfect source of balanced calcium for your pet (if fed ground up as bone meal) and are great for helping to keep teeth healthy and strong when fed raw and whole.

suitable for

dog, cat, ferret

preparation time

Short: 5–15 minutes to prepare.

ingredients

4 chicken wings (use chicken necks for larger dogs)
1 lamb shin
25 g mixed kidney and liver (chicken or beef)

method

The first part of this recipe may need to be prepared by your butcher. Ask to have the bones chopped into 1–2 cm pieces for cats and larger for big dogs.
Chop the liver and kidney coarsely.
Mix the chopped bones together with the liver and kidney.

serve

Serve in individual portions to each of your pets ensuring you keep them company to prevent fighting over this delicacy!

Chicken tagine

suitable for

dog, human

preparation time

Long: over 45 minutes to prepare and cook.

ingredients

1 whole chicken, skin removed, trimmed of fat and cut into 8 pieces
1 tablespoon olive oil
2 garlic cloves, minced
2 carrots, sliced
2 turnips, peeled and sliced
2 celery stalks, sliced
2 small zucchini, sliced
1 teaspoon ground cumin
½ teaspoon ground ginger
3 cups chicken stock
½ cup lemon juice
1 cup cooked chick peas
10 dried dates, sliced
¼ cup chopped fresh coriander

method

Heat the olive oil over medium heat. Fry the garlic.
Add the carrot, turnip, celery and dates, and cook for another couple of minutes.
Add the chicken, ginger, stock and cumin and bring to boil.
Simmer for 45–60 minutes or until the chicken is falling off the bone.
Remove and discard bones.
Add the chickpeas, zucchini and lemon juice and cook for a further 15 minutes.
Stir in coriander. Allow to cool.

serve

Serve with canine couscous (page 20).

Beef and pork bolognese

Human feeding fads and anthropomorphism

We are bombarded by the media with nutritional information for humans on a daily basis. Some of this is science and some are merely marketing ploys. It can be very hard to tell the difference. It is hard enough to decide what should be applied to our own diets let alone trying to apply it to other species. Applying human attributes to other species is called anthropomorphism. We do a lot of this with our animals and it is by no means always a bad thing. We need to be able to empathise with our pets to be able to respond to their needs. At the same time, we must be careful not to apply inappropriate rules to them. Human nutritional advisers suggest that the best source of calcium is dairy products. Usually they mean cows' milk products. But dogs often digest cows' milk products inadequately. The best source of calcium for dogs is raw bones and ground bone meal. Another common anthropomorphic misconception is that multivitamins will provide what a dog needs if the base of the diet is meat. Multivitamins have their place but they do not replace all the nutrients missing from a muscle meat diet.

On the other hand, there are some important nutrients or nutritional medical supplements that have been found to have good effects in certain situations for dogs as well as humans. Balanced omega fatty acids and glucosamine are those that come to mind. The former are often used to reduce the itchiness associated with skin disease. The latter is frequently used in palliative care of arthritic patients. Both should be used under veterinary advice.

Beverages – water the right way

Water is the most important ingredient in your dog's diet. Luckily dogs are not usually fussy about where they drink from. However, it is still important to have plenty of drinking water available in all areas in which your dog may be confined. Some dogs love to play in water. So, it is a good idea to have several sources to make sure they always have a full clean dish somewhere to drink from.

Occasionally, when your dog is ill, you might need to encourage them to drink more. Or you may just have an unusually reluctant drinker. Dogs can have milk but they are not necessarily good at digesting it. From my experience, it is okay to feed your dog recipes that contain milk products as long as you know that they don't have an adverse reaction to them and that they don't form a permanent part of their diet. A better way to increase the fluid intake is to offer soups, stocks and casseroles. I would advise this rather than giving milk on almost every occasion.

The material that a drinking container is made out of is also quite significant. Plastic becomes scratched quickly and gradually gets more difficult to clean. Damaged plastic also seems to cause more rashes around dogs' mouths.

Toto the boxer had a long history of skin disease around his nose and lips, which eventually extended in a rash up to his eyebrows

He was in a terrible state. After many weeks of treatment-trials and investigation, we discovered that we could get rid of the problem by changing all his feeding bowls to ceramic and stainless steel. Poor fellow!

Radar the golden retriever had a drinking problem. He couldn't help splashing it all over the place with his paw or by plunging his whole head into the dish. This wouldn't have been a problem except that he was prone to ear infections and the vet had advised that his ears be kept dry. An innovative choice of water container solved this problem. A long, narrow deep vase firmly anchored to the wall only allowed his nose in. His ears stayed nice and dry.

Milk – good or evil?

Milk is only a good food for mammals of suckling age. Dogs are not designed to digest large quantities of cows' or goats' milk which contain lactose. It is possible to feed milk products that have reduced lactose such as natural yoghurt, aged cheese and low lactose milk. Even feeding milk to a baby mammal is not as easy as it sounds. Cows' milk is appropriate for cows. Milk from a goat, sheep, elephant, monkey, kangaroo and rhinoceros is very different from cows' milk. Zoos and wildlife rehabilitation centres often have to figure out an appropriate recipe for a milk formula to raise baby mammals that either cannot be fed by their parents or are orphaned.

If you find yourself in the situation of having to bottle-rear puppies, kittens or ferret kits, please use the correct commercial milk formula and make it up strictly according to instructions. It is quite detrimental to the health of young animals to be fed the incorrect formula.

Stock

suitable for
dog, cat, ferret, human

preparation time
Long: over 45 minutes to prepare and cook.

ingredients
1 kg mixed bones (beef shin bones, mutton and veal bones)
2 litres water
1 parsnip
1 carrot
4 allspice berries
1 stalk celery
1 teaspoon salt
12 peppercorns (if your pet likes them; they become soft and are not hot)
bunch of herbs (I prefer oregano, parsley and sage for dogs)

method
Wash bones and remove fat from meat. Cut meat finely.
Scoop the marrow out of the bones and keep the bones aside to feed uncooked. Bones should only ever be fed uncooked.
Put meat, marrow, water and salt into stockpot, allow to stand for 30 minutes.
Bring slowly to the boil then skim the fat off the top.
Roughly cut up the vegetables and add them to the stockpot with the herbs.
Simmer on low for at least two hours.
Increase the heat and reduce the stock while stirring if you need it to be stronger.
Allow to cool then strain and refrigerate.
Don't leave whole pieces of vegetable in the stock unless you intend to use it within 24 hours otherwise it may ferment.
Before using, skim fat off the top.

tip
Stock may be frozen.

Party food, treats and snacks

We all love special occasions. Our dogs are no exception. They may not necessarily understand that it is their birthday or Christmas or even just a great day for a picnic but they can certainly appreciate the excitement around them. Tails wag and mouths drool while we cook up a storm or race around packing for a day out. We love to pamper our nearest and dearest with special meals, desserts and treats. Why shouldn't we include our dogs? Here are some ideas on creating safe special treats that your dog will find delicious.

Rita's birthday cake for dogs

Yoghurt-iced birthday cake

suitable for
dog

preparation time
Medium: 15–45 minutes to prepare and cook.

ingredients
500 g minced beef, extra lean
8 eggs
1 cup oatmeal
½ cup dry biscuit crumbs
2 cups natural yoghurt

method
The night before making the cake, strain the yoghurt in muslin over a bowl in the fridge.
Preheat oven to 180 °C.
Blend the mince, eggs, oatmeal and biscuit crumbs until smooth.
Grease oblong cake tin with oil or margarine.
Pour mixture into the tin.
Bake in the oven for 25–30 minutes.
Allow to cool.
Invert onto serving platter and ice the cake with the strained yoghurt.

Rita's birthday cake for dogs

suitable for
dog

preparation time
Medium: 15–45 minutes to prepare and cook.

ingredients
1 kg minced beef
1 carrot, sliced coarsely
1 stick celery, sliced coarsely
1 tablespoon tomato paste
1 cup of gravy made very thick (powdered or home-made gravy)
8 medium-sized potatoes

method
Put the potatoes on to boil.
Stir-fry the minced beef, carrot and celery in a little olive oil until the mince is thoroughly browned.
Make the gravy from the powdered mix or heat the home-made gravy.
Add a tablespoon of tomato paste to the mince and then mix the gravy through.
The mixture should be thick and sticky.
Use a dish as a mould to shape the mince and empty it onto a platter.
Mash the potatoes; add a little low-lactose milk if the mash isn't smooth enough.
Cover the mince cake with a thick layer of mashed potato.
Refrigerate for at least one hour prior to serving.

Lydia's birthday

Rita is a vet nurse at the Lort Smith Animal Hospital. This is what she made for her dog Lydia, a border collie-cross kelpie, on her first birthday. She took Lydia to the pub where she used to work (it was dog friendly at the time) and held a party there for her. She had six human guests and one canine guest. The dogs even tolerated the party hats, which is more than could be said for the humans! The chef was a friend of Rita's and he created a doggy birthday cake that was an absolute winner with the birthday girl, although she only shared it with one guest! Here's the recipe.

Vets, dogs and utes

As newly graduated vets, many of us worked in country towns as our first job. We would travel hundreds of kilometres to meet up and discuss the highs and lows of treating our patients and their owners. Vets, dogs and utes would converge on someone's farm and we would regale each other with fantastic tales of who had the worst midnight calving, longest emergency surgery, longest hours, and of course stories about the animals that had captured our hearts. We would all bring food and drink

Doggy picnic

Beef cakes

This is a great picnic recipe as it is durable and easy to divide no matter how many friends arrive. You do have to cook it before the picnic unless you have a barbeque available at the destination.

suitable for

dog

preparation time

Short: 5–15 minutes to prepare and cook.

ingredients

120 g flour
60 g beef mince
1 teaspoon soy sauce
1 egg
200 ml beef stock
1 tablespoon yoghurt

method

Sift the flour.
Add all the other ingredients. The mince doesn't need to be cooked if you plan to serve the pancakes immediately but it should be cooked if you are going to keep them for a couple of days.
Use the batter to make pancakes as you would normally.

serve

Serve them cool with a little grated fresh parmesan.

tip

Dogs sometimes like them with some spicy chutney (must be onion free).

Steamed vegetables

suitable for

dog, bird, lizard, rodent, human

preparation time

Short: 5–15 minutes to prepare and cook.

ingredients

broccoli florets
cauliflower florets
2 cm cubes carrot
2 cm cubes parsnip

method

Steam the vegetables until just soft enough to pierce with a fork.
Don't let them cook until soggy or else they will make a messy treat.
Allow to cool then pack ready for the picnic.

Fruit salad

Dogs love fruit as long as they are introduced to it at an early age.
Try this recipe for the second course of your picnic. It is people-friendly as well.

suitable for

dog, bird, lizard, rodent, human

preparation time

Short: 5–15 minutes to prepare.

ingredients

apple
banana
mango
cantaloupe

method

Cut the apple, banana, mango and cantaloupe into 2 cm cubes.
Discard the mango seed carefully as they have been known to cause obstructions in the intestines of dogs.
Also discard the skin of the mango, banana and cantaloupe as dogs don't usually like it.
Mix together in a bowl.

serve

Use as individual treats throughout your picnic.

Carnivore gravy

suitable for
dog, cat, ferret

preparation time
Short: 5–15 minutes to prepare and cook.

ingredients
dripping from roasted meat
1 tablespoon sifted flour
200 ml beef or veal stock
100 ml of puréed steamed vegetables

method
Remove meat from roasting dish.
Strain dripping into a basin.
Add flour and brown over low heat.
Mix stock and vegetable purée. Add mixture to pan gradually and stir till boiling.
Reduce heat and continue cooking until gravy thickens.

serve
Serve warm as it smells great to dogs.

Pork rubbings

Spice up your dog's Sunday breakfast with this recipe.

suitable for
dog, cat, ferret

preparation time
Short: 5–15 minutes to prepare and cook.

ingredients
4 pieces bacon
2 eggs
1 cup spinach leaves
black pepper
lemon wedge
1 cup dry food of your dog's choice

method
Fry the bacon until crispy. Drain on kitchen paper but reserve the fat. Allow the fat to cool.
Fry the eggs in another pan.
Wash the spinach leaves and dress with lemon juice and black pepper.
Once the bacon fat has cooled, rub it through the dry dog food.

serve
Serve the eggs, bacon and spinach on the table for yourself.
Serve the dry food and pork rubbings on the floor for your dog.
Eat with gusto. (Your dog is allowed to lick the bowl!)

Flavour enhancers

Dogs love new flavours. They also love to have the chance to eat what you are eating. Use these recipes to spice up some meatballs (page 54), flavour a new pet food, or just as a treat on some bread.

As a special treat, try grinding up some dried fish or some finely chopped fried bacon and sprinkling it over rice. Dogs love the salty taste and the rice reduces their desire to beg for seconds.

Party time

Dude was a little blonde gibbon who arrived at Singapore Zoo clinging to the shoulder of a policeman. The policeman had found him in a suburban street, or rather Dude had found the policeman. Dude had leapt onto the policeman, hugging him for dear life and had taken him quite by surprise. Dude arrived at the zoo wearing a gold necklace, and appeared very fit and friendly. After we examined him we discarded the gold necklace and settled him into a more gibbon-like environment. A week or so later Dude's owner turned up at the zoo in a red sports car. Apparently this chap was a ship's captain and had been given the gibbon in Indonesia because it had lost its parents. Dude had stayed on the ship for a few months and had been fed on galley scraps. He was surprisingly healthy. The only lingering effect of his stint at sea was that he loved a good party atmosphere. He was happiest in crowds of noisy people eating together.

Raw vegetables

suitable for
dog, ferret, bird, rabbit, guinea pig, rodent

preparation time
Short: 5–15 minutes to prepare.

ingredients
carrot and celery sticks
raw cauliflower and broccoli florets

serve
Offer your dog a piece of the raw vegetables that you are cooking for dinner.

tip
Give it to your dog outside the kitchen so she doesn't beg next time! Some dogs may eat it straight away. Some may play with it first. Either way they will be happily entertained while you are preparing dinner.

Sweet roasted vegetables

suitable for
dog, bird, rodent, human

preparation time
Medium: 15–45 minutes to prepare and cook.

ingredients
pumpkin slices
sweet potato slices
carrot
parsnip
capsicum
turnip

method
Preheat the oven to 170 °C.
Place the vegetable slices onto aluminium foil on an oven tray.
Drizzle with olive oil (optional).
Cover with another piece of foil.
Bake for 30 minutes.

tip
This does not freeze well so cook only a small batch at a time.

serve
Serve at room temperature.

Sweet roasted vegetables

Banana and rice arancini

These rice balls were a favourite treat of Dude the gibbon. Dogs love them too.

suitable for
dog, ferret, bird, rodent

preparation time
Medium: 15–45 minutes to prepare and cook.

ingredients
- 1 cup white rice
- 2 eggs
- 6 very ripe Lady Finger bananas (they are sweeter, but you can use the larger ones instead)

method
Boil the unwashed white rice for 15 minutes in rapidly boiling water. (Cook the rice unwashed so it stays stickier.) Allow to cool.

Boil the eggs until firm but still sticky, not runny.

Add all the ingredients to a large mixing bowel and blend thoroughly. This is messy work so you might like to enlist the help of children. They love it!

Shape the mixture into orange-sized balls (or golf ball size if using them for ferrets).

serve
Serve immediately.

tip
These are great to hide medication in, especially if it is sweet syrupy medicine.

Bacon polenta

This dish has strong aromas and is very attractive to dogs. They will drool with anticipation.

suitable for
dog, cat, ferret

preparation time
Long: over 45 minutes to prepare and cook.

ingredients
- 1 cup polenta
- 1 cup chopped bacon
- ½ cup chopped ham
- 3 eggs
- ½ cup low-lactose milk

method
Fry the bacon until crispy.

Add all the other ingredients to the pan. Simmer on the stove for about 25 minutes.

After the mixture thickens add water to dilute and cook for a further 30 minutes.

serve
Serve cooled.

tip
This treat should only be fed in small amounts if your dog has not had bacon or milk before, as it is very rich and fatty.

Banana and rice arancini

Dried heart treats

suitable for
dog, cat, ferret, turtle

preparation time
Long: over 45 minutes to prepare and cook.

ingredients
500 g heart (beef, lamb or pork)
2 crushed garlic cloves

method
Plunge hearts and garlic into a pot of boiling water then reduce to simmer for about 20 minutes or until cooked through.
Remove the meat from the boiled water and allow it to cool until it can be handled.
Preheat oven to 200 °C.
Slice hearts into 1 cm strips and place on a greased baking tray.
Bake for 20–30 minutes.
Allow to cool and store in an airtight container in the fridge.

Bacon and cheese dog biscuits

suitable for
dog

preparation time
Medium: 15–45 minutes to prepare and cook.

ingredients
3 cups whole wheat flour
1 teaspoon garlic salt
½ cup soft bacon fat
1 cup grated cheese
1 egg lightly beaten
1 cup low-lactose milk

method
Preheat oven to 200 °C.
Mix flour and garlic salt in a large bowl.
Stir in bacon fat.
Add cheese and egg. Gradually add enough milk to form dough. Knead dough and roll out to about 2 cm thick.
Use a biscuit shape cutter to cut out dough.
Place on a greased flat oven tray.
Bake for 12 minutes or until the cookies start to brown.

serve
Serve cool.

Bacon and cheese dog biscuits

Vitamins and awful offal

My first job as a vet was in a country practice that serviced mostly cattle enterprises. We had a scattering of emu, ostrich and deer farms as well as dogs, cats and the occasional kangaroo to attend to. Our vet clinic provided the meat inspection service for the local abattoir, so it happened that I began to learn about the human food chain first hand. To be a meat inspector I had to learn all about food hygiene and storage, as well as becoming very well versed in what a well-fed, healthy animal looks like on the inside. This stood me in good stead when I went on to work in zoos and needed to improve kitchen, food preparation and storage facilities. I could also ensure that the meat we were getting was of good quality. I learnt many recipes from the abattoir workers as they told me what could be done with the less familiar parts of the carcass. Sweetbreads, kidneys, brains and others that I won't mention!

In the wild, organ meats are a vital source of vitamins and fat. They contain quite different nutrients compared to muscle meat. Liver is an excellent source of vitamin A. However, animals that are fed liver alone can become severely ill. Vitamins in excess can be just as dangerous as the deficiencies.

Liver hedgehog

suitable for
dog, cat, ferret, turtle

preparation time
Medium: 15–45 minutes to prepare and cook.

ingredients
- 1½ cups oat flour
- 1 cup rolled oats
- 1 cup oat bran
- 2 teaspoons baking soda
- 500 g raw liver
- 2 cloves garlic
- 1 egg lightly beaten

method
Preheat oven to 200 °C.
Blend liver and garlic in a food processor until liquid and smooth. Stir the egg through the liver and garlic.
Mix oat flour, rolled oats, oat bran and baking soda together in separate bowl.
Add batches of the wet ingredients to the dry ingredients. Blend thoroughly.
Grease a flat baking tray.
Pour the mixture onto a tray and smooth down to 2 cm thick.
Bake 10–12 minutes or until firm.
Cut into squares.

serve
Serve cooled.

tip
These biscuits should only be fed occasionally and in small pieces.

Liver hedgehog

Fruit muffins

suitable for
dog, rodent

preparation time
Medium: 15–45 minutes to prepare and cook.

ingredients
1½ cups plain flour
1 cup rolled oats
1 cup oat bran
2 teaspoons baking soda
1 teaspoon cinnamon
1 egg lightly beaten
¼ cup honey
3 tablespoon vegetable oil
¾ cup milk (low-lactose)
½ apple grated
½ banana mashed

method
Preheat oven to 200 °C.
Line muffin tins with baking paper.
Mix dry ingredients.
In a separate bowl mix the egg, honey, oil and fruit.
Add the milk to the dry ingredients and blend well.
Add the other wet ingredients into the batter and mix well.
Distribute the mix evenly between your muffin tins.
Bake for 15–20 minutes.

serve
Serve cooled.

Vegetable muffins

suitable for
dog, rodent

preparation time
Medium: 15–45 minutes to prepare and cook.

ingredients
1½ cups plain flour
1 cup rolled oats
1 cup oat bran
2 teaspoons baking soda
1 teaspoon cumin
¼ cup grated zucchini
¼ cup grated carrot
1 egg lightly beaten
¼ cup honey
3 tablespoons vegetable oil
¾ cup water

method
Preheat oven to 200 °C.
Line muffin tins with baking paper.
In a bowl mix the egg, honey, oil and grated vegetables.
In a separate bowl mix the oat flour, rolled oats, oat bran, baking soda and cumin.
Add the water to these dry ingredients and blend well.
Now add the grated vegetable mix and blend again.
Distribute the mix evenly between your muffin tins.
Bake for 15–20 minutes.

serve
Serve cooled.

Cheese muffins

suitable for
dog, rodent

preparation time
Medium: 15–45 minutes to prepare and cook.

ingredients
1½ cups plain flour
1 cup rolled oats
1 cup oat bran
2 teaspoons baking soda
½ teaspoon dried sage powder
1 egg lightly beaten
50 ml vegetable stock
3 tablespoons vegetable oil
¾ cup water
¼ cup grated mozzarella or cheddar cheese

method
Preheat oven to 200 °C.
Line muffin tins with baking paper.
Mix the oat flour, rolled oats, oat bran, baking soda and sage.
In a separate bowl mix the egg, vegetable stock, oil and cheese.
Add the water to the dry ingredients and blend well.
Add the other wet ingredients into the batter and mix well.
Distribute the mix evenly between muffin tins.
Bake for 15–20 minutes.

serve
Serve cooled.

Vegetable muffins

Chicken and date muffins

suitable for
dog

preparation time
Medium: 15–45 minutes to prepare and cook.

ingredients
¼ cup shredded chicken (cooked)
1½ cups wholemeal flour
1 cup rolled oats
1 cup oat bran
2 teaspoons baking soda
½ teaspoon dried oregano
1 egg lightly beaten
1 cup chicken stock
3 tablespoon vegetable oil
¾ cup water
4 chopped dates (soak in warm stock first)

method
Preheat oven to 200 °C.
Line muffin tins with baking paper.
Mix the oat flour, rolled oats, oat bran, baking soda and oregano.
In a separate bowl mix the egg, chicken stock, oil, chicken and dates.
Add the water to the dry ingredients and blend well.
Add the other wet ingredients into the batter and mix well.
Distribute the mix evenly between muffin tins.
Bake for 15–20 minutes.

serve
Serve cooled.

Pancakes

suitable for
dog

preparation time
Short: 5–15 minutes to prepare and cook. My cat actually loves these pancakes too but prefers to eat the filling separately.

ingredients
batter
120 g flour
1 egg
250 ml water
1 tablespoon yoghurt
salt

filling
120 g of pork mince
2 teaspoon flour
4 tablespoons stock (use stock on page 28)
1 teaspoon soy sauce
4 chopped dried apricots

method
Sift the flour and salt.
Mix into a batter with the water, egg and yoghurt.
Stir-fry the mince and chopped dried apricots until the mince is golden brown and then add the flour, stock and Worcestershire sauce. Bring to the boil, then reduce heat to simmer for 5 minutes.
Make the pancakes. Spread the meat mixture on them and roll up.
Share if you dare!

serve
Serve cold.

Chicken and date muffins

Food as entertainment

We all know that food can be used as a reward when training dogs and that sometimes you can keep a dog entertained and distracted for a few hours with a nice meaty bone. But did you know that there is a whole field of science called enrichment? It refers to the specific discipline of providing entertainment and mental stimulation for animals. Many methods of enrichment involve food in some way. We use it extensively in zoos and it can also be applied to your dogs at home. Sometimes it involves hiding food in places from which it is time consuming for your dog to extract it. Other methods use food scents to make a treasure hunt. Many of the recipes and suggestions are highly versatile and adaptable. Don't be afraid to experiment but remember to include any enrichment treats in the daily allowance so that your dogs diet remains balanced.

While you're out

What do our dogs do while we are out? Brutus the boxer used to chew the garden furniture. Max the staffy used to climb the fence and look for his owner. Jasmine the Samoyed used to scale the fence, brave the water buffalo in the paddock next door and go to visit the neighbours.

One of the reasons that dogs misbehave while we are out is that what is going on elsewhere looks better than at home. Here are some ideas on how to enrich your dogs' home environment. They all involve food as this is a cook book, but there is plenty of information out there suggesting other ways you can provide enrichment for your dog.

Apple bobbing

suitable for
dog

preparation time
Short: 5–15 minutes to prepare.

ingredients
apples (for large dogs)
dried liver (for non fruit eaters)

method
Place the fruit into a tub of water.
Play with him to show him the way to get the fruit out.
Leave him to it when you're out.

Scent trail

suitable for
dog, cat

preparation time
Short: 5–15 minutes to prepare.

ingredients
fresh liver
liver treats (page 96)
anchovy oil (page 98)

method
Crush the liver into a paste.
Crush the liver treats into a powder.

serve
Use one of these to make a scent trail around the garden by smearing or sprinkling it onto logs, branches and leaves erratically around the garden. Just a little will do; dogs have a powerful sense of smell.

tip
Change the scent used each day.

Dogs feeling poorly

Aahh! This is what nurturing your beautiful pet is all about. There is nothing more rewarding than convincing a sick pet to start eating again when they haven't eaten for days. It signals such hope and victory, and shows that they have regained the will to recover. Vets and owners have all sorts of tricks up their sleeves to encourage inappetent animals to eat and to encourage fussy patients to eat the right thing for their illness.

There are many valid reasons for either changing a diet or having a diet that differs from the ideal recommended for a particular species. Medical conditions such as kidney or liver disease, diabetes, food intolerances, metabolic disorders and recovery from illness can be reason enough to require strict dietary management. Availability of ingredients and the quality of those ingredients available can be another reason for changes to a diet. On the other hand, a diet may need to be rectified if there is a history of feeding an unbalanced menu to a dog. A diet may also need to be changed due to obesity or weight loss. Before changing the diet of a dog that is ill or has rapidly lost or gained weight, the patient needs to undergo veterinary examination. Dietary management can often be the solution but medical management may also be necessary.

Wesley the beagle

Wesley the beagle suffered from problems with his adrenal glands. This in turn caused his liver to have to work too hard. Originally all that we could see wrong with him was that his coat was a little dull and coarse and he was often anxious. His body's resources seemed exhausted and this can lead to a decrease in its natural immune defences. His owner was pursuing the appropriate medical path with us but wanted to do more for Wesley while we were waiting on a diagnosis. We looked for special treats and supplements that would provide the nutrients that Wesley was likely to be using the most during his illness.

Wesley the beagle had this liver tonic as a side dish to his main meal each day. He loved it and continued to have it even after his medical problem was addressed.

Liver support tonic

suitable for

dog

preparation time

Short: 5–15 minutes to prepare.

ingredients

2 carrots
½ a cucumber
1 apple
2 tablespoons lemon juice

method

Juice the vegetables and keep the pulp to use in a meatloaf (page 6) for your dog as a source of fibre. Many dogs love the juice by itself. Because it is tangy some dogs curl their lips back as if in distaste, but they still drink it. 20 g raw liver blended to a paste and mixed into the juice can improve the flavour for dogs if they are hesitant.

You may also add various herbal supplements. We used purified milk thistle (also called St Mary's thistle) for Wesley. You should get advice from a vet interested in herbal medicine on dose rates appropriate for your dog as they can be quite different from dose rates for people.

Dry food meatballs

suitable for

dog

preparation time

Short: 5–15 minutes to prepare.

ingredients

500 g minced beef
2 cups dry dog food
¼ cup of honey
¼ cup wheat germ oil

method

Grind dry dog pellets in food processor or blender.
Mix all ingredients together, and then roll into balls.
Freeze individually then store together in freezer.
Defrost as needed.

Restricted protein arancini

These treats can be used for dogs that are on a diet with moderately restricted protein. Dogs with early renal failure require restricted protein. If your dog is sick, please ask your vet before feeding any home-cooked recipes.

suitable for

dog

preparation time

Medium: 15–45 minutes to prepare and cook.

ingredients

115 g minced beef
1 large hard boiled egg
2 cups cooked rice, unwashed without salt
75 g bread crumbs
1 tablespoon vegetable oil

method

Dry-fry the minced beef in a non-stick pan.
Mix the minced beef, its juices and the rice together. You may add a little water to make the mix stickier.
Cut the egg into quarters.
Mould the mince mix around each piece of egg and then roll them in bread crumbs.
Heat the oil gently and cook the arancini over low heat, moving them frequently to ensure even cooking.

serve

Serve when cool.

Mince and rice

suitable for

dog

preparation time

Medium: 15–45 minutes to prepare and cook.

ingredients

500 g lean minced meat (chicken or beef is used most commonly. Ideally you should choose a meat that your pet has not been fed before.)
2 cups white rice
1 tablespoon unflavoured Metamucil (soluble dietary fibre available in chemists)

method

Bring a saucepan of water to the boil.
Add the rice and boil for 15 minutes.
Meanwhile dry-fry the mince in a non-stick pan.
Drain any excess fat.
Mix the mince and rice together. Only use the Metamucil for dogs that no longer have diarrhoea.

serve

Feed when cooled.

tip

May be stored frozen in portions and defrosted either in the fridge overnight or the microwave. Beware of overheating in the microwave.

Upset tummies

Some animals suffer food intolerances. Jasmine, my old Samoyed, suffered from a bowel upset that wouldn't go away. She was bright and happy, but eventually it was going to sap her resources. It was also very unbecoming on her long white fur! It turned out that she had a condition called chronic inflammatory bowel disease. She became very sensitive to many ingredients in her diet. The treatment required her to eat a highly restricted prescription dry food with added fibre and very specific proteins. We were to refrain from giving any other food at all to allow her to recover. This meant she wasn't even allowed to have her daily fresh bread roll from the bakery! She was fed solely this diet for twelve months and then was slowly reintroduced to a more varied diet. The day she was given her first bread roll again by the baker, the poor darling was quite sure someone would try to take it from her. She outran us all the way home with it delicately held between her teeth, to eat it undisturbed.

While the initial medical investigation was taking place, Jasmine was fed a very bland mince and rice diet that helped keep her diarrhoea under control. This was not a balanced diet and hence was only a short-term solution. Vets often use variations of this recipe to assist dog and sometimes cat recoveries from intestinal upsets due to garbage-indigestion.

Beef meatballs (page 64)

Liver support tonic (page 54)

Chicken stock and chicken soup

Some animals don't cope very well with particular types of meat or even specific fats. I've seen jungle cats with gurgling tummies and loose stools when they were given fatty lamb. Domestic cats can also develop food intolerances. This can present as a tummy upset, and the body tries to rid itself of the offending ingredient by the closest exits. Most unpleasant for all concerned! Some dogs develop pancreatitis (a painful condition that causes vomiting and general misery) after eating a fatty meal. This recipe for chicken soup is low fat and is good for animals that suffer from these types of tummy upsets. It is also a tasty dinner for any healthy, happy dog, ferret or cat.

suitable for

dog, cat, ferret

preparation time

Long: over 45 minutes to prepare and cook.

ingredients

1 whole chicken, skin and viscera removed
1 tablespoon finely grated fresh ginger or a 2 cm cube of ginger
1 carrot
1 stick celery
2 cloves garlic
1 teaspoon salt
bunch of coriander and lime leaves

method

You can chop the chicken coarsely and wait for the meat to fall off the bones to make stock in the same way as the red meat stock described opposite or you can use the chicken whole like this.
Place the piece of ginger, lime and coriander leaves inside the chicken.
Cut the carrot and celery coarsely and bruise the peeled garlic with the back of a knife.
Rub the sesame oil and the salt into the outside of the chicken.
Place all of this into a large stock pot or saucepan with enough water to cover it.
Bring to the boil, then turn down the heat and simmer for another 30 minutes.
To preserve the stock remove the chicken, strain the remainder and store separately from the solids.
The chicken can then be sliced and used either in the stock as soup or separately.
Discard cooked bones.

Food that animals manage to find for themselves in the wild can be very different to what we can offer them in captivity. With cat and dog diets we are very lucky to have pet food companies that have invested in a huge body of research to develop well-balanced diets that are easy to feed pets. It isn't so easy when the pet is something more unusual or if the animal is captive wildlife.

In the late 1990s I was working in Singapore and had to go to Kalimantan to examine and treat a sick orangutan, Siswi, at a rehabilitation station operated by Orangutan Foundation International and founded by Dr Biruté Galdikas. Siswi was very important to Biruté as she was the adult daughter of one of the first orangutans that Biruté had rehabilitated and released into the wild in Kalimantan. It was thought that Siswi had an abdominal tumour. She was rapidly declining in health and there was no local veterinary service capable of dealing with primates at the time. Biruté and I had met in Singapore and she asked me to fly over to help her try to save Siswi. I had limited equipment but with the help of a machine borrowed from a zoo in Java, we were able to take some X-rays of Siswi. The local hospital developed them for us and we discovered that the mass that we could feel was somewhere in the vicinity of her ovaries.

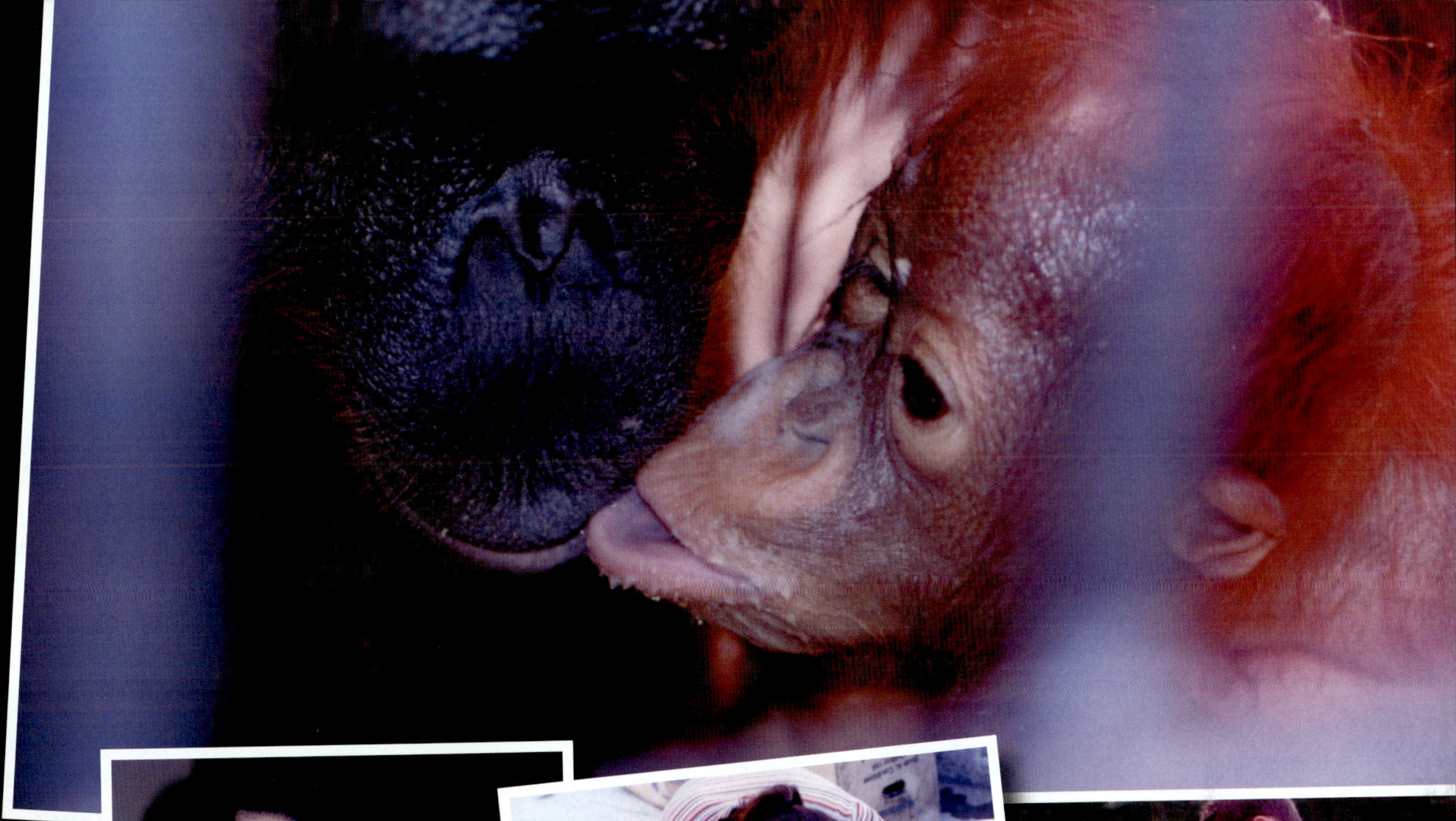

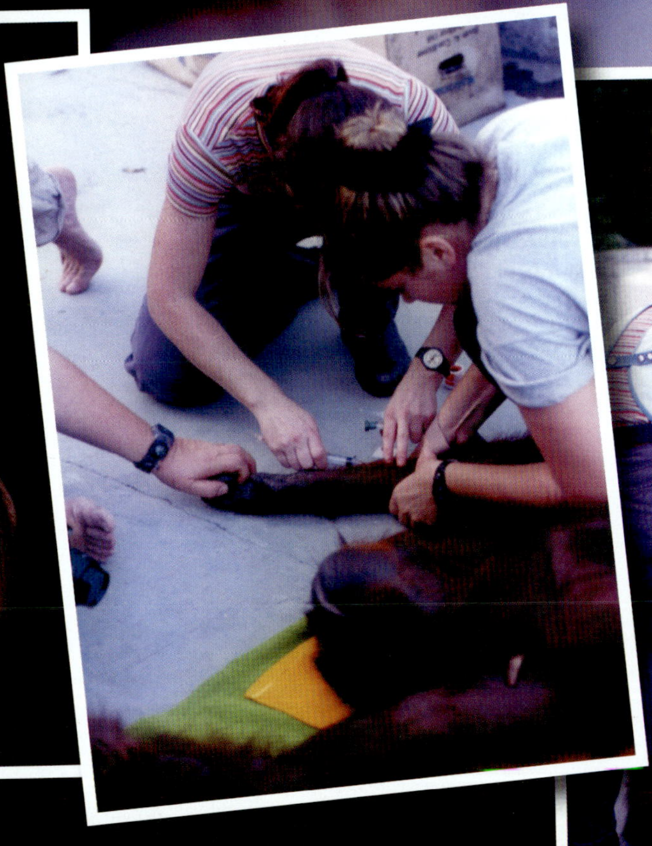
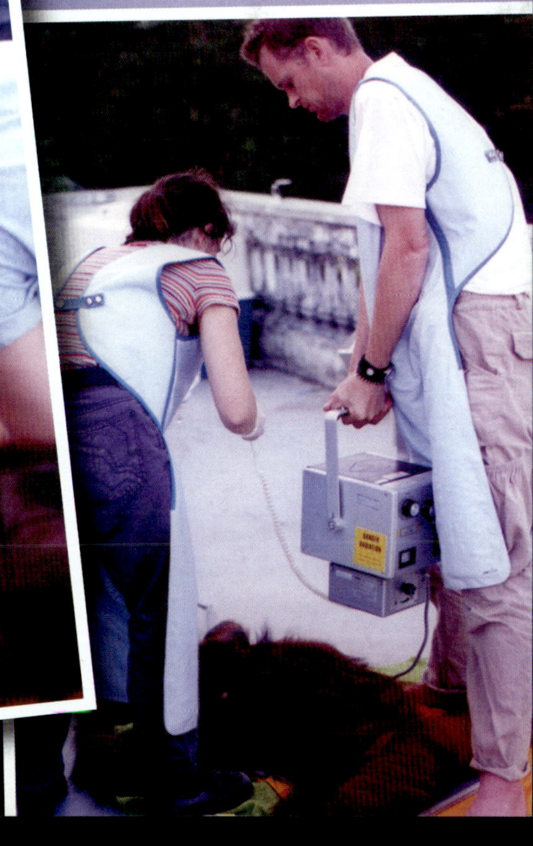

Siswi's surgery

I had to operate as Siswi had been unable to eat and was becoming weaker day by day.

We set up a makeshift theatre on the roof of Biruté's house where we could prevent other orangutans coming to see what was going on. The heat and humidity were intense. So, to avoid our patient overheating, we had to start early in the morning. With the assistance of two student researchers taking the role of nurses, I discovered the source of Siswi's problem. The mass was due to a many-layered infection around her intestines. It was possible to patch this up but not to remove it entirely.

Siswi's recovery

The difficulty we faced as she woke up was how to feed her during her recovery. We couldn't tube feed her as she was semi-wild and would not tolerate any direct contact. She had to eat immediately or she would have no nutritional building blocks with which to heal. However, she could not eat a bulky diet as it would not pass safely through her surgical site.

As I started to develop a recovery diet for Siswi I looked into the diet of both the young orangutans undergoing rehabilitation (rescued from the illegal pet trade) at the station and also at the food items that wild orangutans browse. The easiest fruit to get in bulk was surprisingly familiar to me but not at all like what wild orangutans had access to locally. Apples, oranges and bananas were readily available but it wasn't easy to get local jungle fruits. It is a situation that is familiar to keepers of wildlife in captivity throughout the world, be they pets, display animals or rehabilitated wildlife such as Siswi. We often make do with the ingredients we have available but it is important to seek expert advice on how to meet the species' daily nutrient requirements when formulating a complete home cooked diet, especially when an animal is ill or recovering from surgery. Please ask your vet for advice on complete diets and diets appropriate for particular illnesses.

Siswi did recover but she did not go back into the jungle to fend for herself. However, she was able to continue raising her baby and was free to come and go as she chose.

Medication

Consider the effect your animal's medication is having on the digestion of food and how it changes what is available to be absorbed by the body. Diets can be altered accordingly and medication given in various ways to reduce side effects.

Bessie, a doe-eyed Cavalier King Charles spaniel, came in to me with an upset tummy. She had recently started heart medication and although she had regained her wriggly joyful self for a while she started to become quiet and miserable again after a week. Bessie's human told me she couldn't find anything that would tempt Bessie. The timing of her dinner turned out to be the key. She needed to have a full stomach to be able to tolerate her medication. I arranged for her to be given her dinner just before her medication. Now she's bouncing around again.

Beef meatballs

Finding something to entice your dog to eat should be easier than getting jungle fruit for Siswi. If you know their habits and their history you'll know whether they prefer wet casserole style food, loaf style food or dry food. Have a think about what really made them come begging, whether or not they were allowed to!

These little meat balls are generally a success. They are easy to feed to your dog and don't require too much chewing. You can give them throughout the day if your pet is only eating a little at a time. They are a little fatty so don't give them to patients suffering pancreatitis or gastrointestinal disease.

suitable for

dog, cat, ferret, turtle, lizard, human

preparation time

Medium: 15–45 minutes to prepare and cook.

ingredients

120 g cooked meat (yesterday's roast, without the bones, works well)
chopped parsley and sage
130 ml stock
30 g flour
4 tablespoons dried breadcrumbs
1 egg
extra flour
1 tablespoon olive oil

method

Mince the meat finely.
Mix in saucepan with flour, herbs, and stock. Stir over medium heat until thick.
Allow to cool then use teaspoon-sized amounts formed into balls.
Roll in flour. Dip into the beaten egg.
Roll in breadcrumbs.
Fry in a little olive oil.

serve

Serve when cooled.

tip

These little meatballs are easy to transport and are great to take along as treats for your dog if you are going out together. Cats also love them, especially if you add a little fresh grated parmesan to the breadcrumbs.

Chicken polpettini

suitable for
dog, cat, ferret, turtle, lizard, human

preparation time
Short: 5–15 minutes to prepare and cook.

ingredients
125 g chicken mince
30 g parmesan cheese
1 teaspoon finely grated parmesan cheese
4 tablespoon bread crumbs
salt
1 tablespoon chopped catmint or ordinary mint
1 teaspoon olive oil

method
Mix chicken mince, parmesan, bread crumbs and herbs together with a pinch of salt.
Take a teaspoon of mixture and roll into a ball.
Once all the polpettini are made heat the olive oil in a pan.
Cook the polpettini in batches, gently shaking the pan during cooking until they are golden brown all over.
Alternatively, these meatballs can be braised in 1 cm of boiling water. Braising, rather than cooking in oil, reduces the amount of fat in the polpettini.

serve
Serve cooled.

tip
These little treats may be frozen separately in an ice-cube tray and then stored together in a bag. Defrost them individually to give as rewards or to use as pill-pockets if your dog or cat needs medication.

Nursing Lady back to health

Lady the Rhodesian ridgeback had been terribly constipated. She was miserable. Despite having been treated for her constipation in hospital, she still would not eat or drink. We had a dilemma. We couldn't let her go home until we knew she would eat but perhaps she just wasn't eating because she was away from her family. She looked at us with big sad eyes no matter what we put in front of her.

Eventually, I went into her cage with her and sat down. She leaned on me while I patted her heavy head. I offered her some mince and rice which she sniffed with interest but didn't eat. I moulded some together into little balls and offered her one. Again she sniffed with interest but returned her mournful gaze to me without eating. In desperation, I held one to my mouth and pretended to eat it. Then I offered her one again. She ate it with relish! It took a long time to get her to eat the lot as she refused to eat unless I joined her at each mouthful. Cuddling, comforting and pampering are just as important as giving the right medicine to a sick dog.

Storybook feeding

Overindulgence causes unbalanced diets and is dangerous for any species, not just us. Working in a cat and dog practice I have seen many active, well-loved but malnourished dogs. It is often a case of misplaced love, really. Big tough dogs are often fed only muscle meat and maybe some bones because the owners feel this is what a strong dog should be fed. This is what I call storybook feeding.

A sick little gibbon (a long-limbed primate that swings and almost seems to fly through the treetops of South-East Asian jungles) was presented to me when I was working at Singapore Zoo, as the owner could no longer keep him. She didn't know that it was illegal to keep these animals as pets and had tried her best to care for him. Carlos, as we called him, was a contracted little fellow with terribly soft dull hair, and he was only able to move by scooting around on his bottom. I asked the owner what his diet had been and she told me 'bananas'. I asked her what else. She said, 'Oh, he didn't like bread'. She had never considered that he might need to eat other types of food. Unlike the storybook version of the generic monkey, gibbons eat a wide variety of leaves, reasonably low-sugar fruit, plus the occasional lizard and some insects and grubs. A diet with only one or two ingredients is inadequate trees, although he never managed to 'fly' like healthy gibbons.

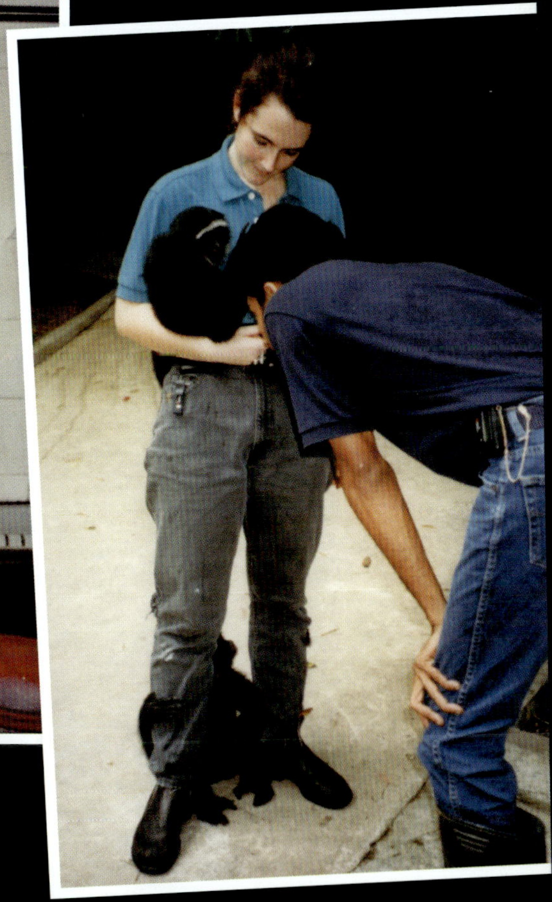

Prescription diets

There will be occasions where your dog has a medical condition that requires the diet to be either restricted or supplemented. Sometimes it can be too complex to meet your dog's needs using wholefoods prepared at home. A prescription diet is often the answer. But how do you convince him to eat it? In this situation, you need to introduce your dog gradually to the new diet. They are fussier than usual when they are ill, and yet because of their condition it is even more important that you follow the veterinary recommendations about diet. If your dog already eats tinned, loaf or dry food then you can use the gradual substitution method. On the first day add a tablespoon of the new food and leave out a tablespoon of the old food. It is best to add dry to dry or wet to wet as they often don't like the two types mixed. Repeat this on the following day. Every second day reduce the amount of the old diet and increase the amount of the new diet by one tablespoon. Eventually they will only be eating the prescription diet.

There are some other methods if your dog flatly refuses to eat the new food and picks it out, so don't despair. Try smearing your hands with bacon fat (wait till it cools, don't burn yourself!) and rubbing it over both the new and the old food to obscure the scent of the offending ingredient. Use the gradual introduction method described above. Once your dog is eating solely prescription diet, wean him off the bacon scent. Don't use fat if your dog is prone to pancreatitis or needs a fat-restricted diet.

For those dogs that prefer casserole or loaf-style food, try soaking the dry food in unsalted stock (page 28) with the fat skimmed off. Then mix the new stock-soaked food with the old food. Serving it slightly warm can improve the aroma.

You can also try making dry food meatballs. Remember, they are not the same as the prescription diet so it is only for the transition period.

He's just fluffy! Caring for overweight dogs

The topic of overweight dogs needs to be addressed delicately. We address this issue with a lot of human emotion and tend to transfer these feelings to discussion about the weight of our animals. Firstly, how do you know if your dog is overweight? What weight should he be? How can you tell if it is just his body shape or if it is really fat? Can a disease be causing your dog to be gaining weight? Lastly and most importantly, will it hurt my dog to be overweight?

Yes, it will hurt your dog to be overweight. Excess weight creates undue wear and tear on the body. Overweight animals are more prone to heart problems, arthritis, skin disease and are generally unable to get up and enjoy playing as much as their slimmer mates. Older animals that suffer from arthritis, breathing difficulties, heart problems and other diseases suffer more if they are overweight because of the heavy load they have to carry around constantly. It's like forcing them to wear a backpack all the time and you wouldn't do that to your arthritic mother, would you? That is why we need to know how to determine if a dog is overweight and how to resolve the problem if he is. For some breeds a range of standard weights are available. However, I find the determination of body condition score and a weight chart of the individual animal's weight fluctuations to be more useful.

You should always be able to feel your dog's ribs through the skin. They should not feel as if they are right under your fingertips but have a bit of flesh over them between the skin and the rib. You should also be able to feel the points of the hips. If you cannot feel these then your dog is overweight. Dogs should also always have a waistline no matter what breed they are. Look down on your pet from above. There should be a narrowing to the waist just below the end of the ribs. This is true even for the more barrel shaped breeds like Staffordshire bull terriers and Rottweilers. Long-haired breeds are harder to assess by sight but the same rules apply. You just need to use your hands to assess body condition. If you can't feel a waistline then he isn't just fluffy!

Can disease cause my dog to be overweight?

This is a question that needs to be discussed with your vet. The vet will be able to help you assess whether the weight of your dog is due to fat accumulation or other causes.

Diseases such as heart-failure and liver-failure can cause a build up of fluid in the wrong places in your dog's body. The tummy can become swollen and bloated and give the appearance of weight gain.

Certain diseases and medications can cause an increase in your pet's appetite, but an animal cannot become fat without being given more food to eat!

How can I tell if I'm feeding too much?

The most common cause of a dog being overweight is overfeeding. Most of our dogs are much smaller than us and require correspondingly less food. They also have different feeding requirements. If your dog has become less active for any reason then he will gain weight if still fed the same amount, even if that is what he has always been fed.

My rule is to look at the body condition. Discuss the feeding history. Make a food diary. Get everyone in the household involved. The more people there are involved in feeding a pet the more likely it is to get out of control. It is easy to forget that scraps are food.

Keep this diary for two weeks. Return to your vet and discuss whether this is a balanced diet. If the overall balance is ok the next step is to reduce the amount in a way that you, your dog and other household members can cope with. Feeding is the way to your dog's heart, but you should not be ruled by your dog's demands to be fed or make your dog sick because of it. It is a delicate balance.

Once you have developed the plan for how much to feed your pet and how often, you need to stick to it. Involve everyone in the house and the neighbours too if you need to! A diet doesn't mean treats must be completely abolished, but it does mean healthy, non-fatty, non-sugary treats. Look at the vegetable treats on page 36 for help. Develop new games and physical rewards rather than feeding. When your pet begs, give her a cuddle, a scratch or grab her favourite toy and have a play. As with people, weight loss for pets also involves exercise. Speak to your vet or go to your local book shop for some ideas. And if you do feed something extra, remember to remove the same amount from the main meal. Continue filling in the feed chart. It will help prevent your plan slipping.

Weigh-ins at your local vet clinic can also play an important part. Involving someone else will give you incentive to continue the program. Praise is just as important to us as it is to our pets!

An example of an overweight dog's food diary

Day	Item fed and how much (in metric cups, teaspoons or tablespoons)				
Sunday	1/3 cup bacon rind	1 bread roll	2 cups dry food 1 fried egg	2 cups dry food	1 cup leftover spaghetti and meat sauce
Monday	1 slice toast	2 cups dry food	¼ cup leftover cereal and milk	2 cups dry food beef	2 cups left over roast
Tuesday					
Wednesday					
Thursday					
Friday					
Saturday					

Food that dogs should avoid

I find that one of the safest ways to start creating new and interesting treats and meals for your pet is to cross off what you can't feed. Each pet species has a unique digestive system and metabolism. A cat requires a diet high in animal protein but this diet would be toxic to a rabbit. Some tortoises kept as pets in Asia and America are herbivorous but a pelleted diet created for them would cause a carnivorous turtle to swell and its shell to turn inside-out. Humans can happily eat an avocado and Spanish onion sandwich but the avocado would be toxic to a bird and the onions toxic to a dog. We need to know what ingredients are toxic for each species.

Chocolate

Chocolate is highly toxic to dogs.

Imagine this scene. It is 2 am on Easter Eve and the kids are finally sound asleep. The Easter Bunny has been and gone and there are brightly glittering foil wrapped eggs and other goodies sparkling in the moonlight on the floor and scattered around the house and garden. Lucy the Maltese terrier gets out of her basket to investigate. She has a sniff of these interesting objects and realises it's party time. By 4 am she is feeling very sick. She is shaking and twitching and has started to cry. By 5 am she has convinced her owners to take her to a veterinary emergency centre. Lucy recovers but spends 24 hours in hospital and the family can't enjoy their Easter dinner without her. At the Lort Smith Animal Hospital we see such cases more often at Easter and Christmas, but also after dinner parties and birthday parties.

The toxic compound in chocolate causes nervous system excitement which may even lead to seizures, cardiac arrhythmias and death. 115 g of milk chocolate can be enough to cause symptoms in a 15 kg dog. Dark chocolate is even more potent.

Onions, leek, garlic, chives

Dogs are extremely sensitive to onion toxicity so it is best to avoid feeding onions in any quantities. Onions cause a particular type of anaemia due to damage to the red blood cells of dogs.

The following shows how little onion is required to cause illness. The toxic dose can be as low as 15–30 g/kg in dogs. If onions are fed at a level greater than 0.5% of your animal's body weight then toxic effects are always noted. A chihuahua would need 30 g of onion or more. A labrador of 30 kg would need 450 g or more. However, to be safe I would not include any in your dog recipes.

Other *allium* species such as leek, chives and garlic can also be toxic but only in large amounts, which is why it is safe to use a little garlic in some of the recipes in this book.

Mushrooms

Do not allow your dog to eat wild mushrooms when out for a walk. There are many possible toxic effects and it is difficult to identify which mushrooms are safe.

Grapes

Grapes and raisins have recently been found to cause vomiting, shaking and acute renal failure. Their toxic properties have not been fully examined. Meanwhile, it is best not to feed them in any amount.

Corn cobs

Corn cobs, especially those divided into smaller pieces, can be lethal to dogs. It is not that the sweet corn is toxic in any way but the fact that dogs can swallow them whole. The cob becomes lodged in the intestines of the poor dog and has to be removed surgically.

Cooked bones

Tyson the Staffordshire bull terrier had been to a barbeque with his mates. It was an exciting time for people and animals alike and everyone felt a little sick the next day. In fact, Tyson felt really terrible. He couldn't keep any food down and had even continued vomiting when he wasn't fed anything. When his owner tried to pick him up to comfort him he yelped in pain. It turned out that Tyson had been eating the discarded lamb chop bones on the ground at the barbeque. They had become lodged in his small intestine. Luckily for Tyson, his owners were able to get him to a veterinary hospital for surgery before the damage was too great. The bones were removed and Tyson rapidly recovered.

Please don't feed cooked bones to your dogs or cats. They are very likely to splinter and the sharp ends can become lodged anywhere from the back of the mouth to the large intestine. Raw bones are an excellent source of calcium and are far less likely to become stuck.

cats

what do cats need?

76
Meals

86
Beverages

90
Party food, treats and snacks

95
Food as entertainment

99
Cats feeling poorly

106
Food that cats should avoid

Domestic cats are often fussy creatures when looked at from a human or canine point of view. They prefer routine over variety. They are fastidious about their own cleanliness and demand the same of their environment. How often has your cat cried by her bowl of water until you wash it and refill it with fresh water? They expect you to know that they prefer their food served at room temperature and like to eat it immediately. Dry food may be left out for them but don't ask them to eat it if it becomes moist or if it is mixed with any other food. They will tolerate new food but only if it is introduced gradually without any pressure! Of course there are exceptions to the rule. A cat that is raised with a varied diet or that has had to fend for himself for a while will often cope better with dietary change. Then there are also cats that think they are dogs and will placidly accept anything served up to them and even raid the garbage.

Having described how fussy cats are, you may wonder why I am including any recipes for them. I have discovered that cats love to cook! Well, they love to be part of the cooking while it's happening. They will hold out a little hooked paw ready to grasp any titbits that come close enough. They will miaow and circle and rub against legs. Do you know why? Their appetite is heavily dependent on their strong sense of smell. A cat that cannot smell very rapidly loses interest in eating, and once cats have stopped eating they often seem to forget how to start again.

So dust off your apron and ask your cat to vacate the kitchen bench. It's time to prepare an aromatic feast for your feline friend.

Cats are strict carnivores. This means that some of their nutrients can be obtained only from animal sources. However, being a carnivore doesn't mean that all of the nutrients need to be from animal products or that a carnivorous animal could survive eating muscle meat only.

A wild carnivore such as a lion will kill and eat an antelope. It will lick the hair off and chew on the skin. The organs are consumed, including the stomach contents with all the partly digested grass, leaves and other grazed plant materials. Last of all, the bones are eaten too. Every part of the prey is needed to provide the long and complex list of essential nutrients that are necessary for the hunter's body to perform at its peak. If we feed only mince or pieces of meat to our carnivorous pets they will become very sick indeed.

Carnivores are fascinating. They are so diverse. A tiger and a lion may have similar requirements for prey but a hyena eats and needs a whole array of other plant-based ingredients in its diet. The king cobra is a carnivore that eats only other snakes! Cats and dogs are also very different in their needs.

Beef tartare (page 78)

Meals

Cats need more animal protein and fat than dogs and cannot survive on an omnivorous diet. Much of the cat's energy supply is derived from fats, whereas dogs obtain most of their energy from carbohydrates. Many dogs will happily snack on carrots and apples but there aren't many cats that would see these as anything other than toys. Then again, there are many labradors that take the term omnivorous too far and will even eat your socks, shoes and couch! Cats are far more likely to look disdainfully at you as you offer them a piece of some new delicacy. Then they might deign to sniff it, taste a little with the tip of their tongue and finally eat it if it proves satisfactory. However, I have also known cats to eat odd things like woollen jumpers, stockings and tinsel, and it does them no good at all!

A cat's dinner

Mate is an adopted cat whose owner works as a vet nurse at the Lort Smith Animal Hospital. Before Mate was adopted she'd been fed a very poor quality diet. Her new owner wanted to feed her a raw food diet. He knew that it was going to be difficult to make the diet balanced. The solution was to include the cat in his shopping list whenever he went to market. Whenever he prepared her a raw food dinner he juiced or blended a small amount of each of the vegetables he had bought for the week and used it in her meal. She ate this food with great relish and grew into a healthy cat with a lovely shiny coat. Interestingly, he discovered that her coat became greasy if he fed her too much meat and not enough vegies.

Here is a recipe based on fresh uncooked ingredients that may appeal to your cat (and probably your ferret and your dog too).

Mate's raw food dinner

suitable for

cat, dog, ferret, turtle, lizard

preparation time

Short: 5–15 minutes to prepare.

ingredients

100 g fresh lean beef mince
½ teaspoon fish oil
3 g bone meal (you can get this from some health food shops)
2 teaspoons chopped fresh liver
¼ carrot, juiced
¼ cup cauliflower, broccoli and parsnip pieces

method

Process the cauliflower, broccoli and parsnip pieces into a paste with the carrot juice.
Mix the mince, liver and bone meal together.
Add the vegies and the fish oil to the meat.
Mix all the ingredients together thoroughly.

serve

Serve at room temperature.

Beef tartare

suitable for

cat, dog, ferret, lizard, turtle

preparation time

Medium: 15–45 minutes to prepare.

ingredients

300 g lean beef steak
1 bacon rasher
¼ zucchini
¼ celery stick
1 garlic clove
1 teaspoon olive oil
½ peeled apple

method

Slice the beef and the bacon very finely. Then slice it again until it almost resembles a mince.
Mince the vegetables the same way.
Grate the apple.
Mix the meat, vegetables, apple and olive oil together by hand.
Mould into shape with a cup-sized serving dish.

serve

Serve raw at room temperature.

Pussycat ravioli

suitable for
cat, dog, ferret

preparation time
Long: over 45 minutes to prepare and cook.

ingredients
pasta
300 g fine white flour
3 eggs

filling
300 g minced chicken
1 garlic clove minced
1 tablespoon olive oil
½ cup finely grated fresh parmesan

method
Sift the flour.
Beat the eggs gently and then pour them into the middle of the flour.
Mix by hand and then knead until smooth and elastic.
Cover the dough in cling wrap and place in the fridge for half an hour.
Gently fry the garlic and minced chicken until golden. Allow to cool.
Mix with the cheese. Refrigerate mix.
Sprinkle flour over a bench top.
Roll out the pasta dough until very thin.
Cut the sheet into several equal sections making sure that you end up with an even number.
Place half teaspoons of the filling at 5 cm intervals across half of the pasta.
Cover with the other half. Gently press down between portions of filling.
Sprinkle lightly with some more flour.
Cut ravioli into individual segments.
Place on lightly floured baking paper and refrigerate or freeze in single layers.
Your ravioli is ready to go.
To cook the ravioli, bring a large pot of water to the boil. Add a generous pinch of salt.
Lower the ravioli in one-by-one and keep them moving to stop them sticking.
Boil until tender.

serve
Serve individually at room temperature with a little parmesan cream (page 85) or anchovy oil (page 98).

Pussycat ravioli

Fishing cats

Fishing cats are wild Asian felids about three to four times the size of our average domestic cats. They are well-named because they do indeed fish both in the wild and in captivity if given the opportunity. The Fishing cats that I have worked with in zoos have been fed a variety of defrosted frozen fish as part of their diet. Zoos have to be diligent with the vitamin supplements they feed to piscivores (fish eaters) as fish rapidly loses its thiamine content when stored. Live fish has good vitamin levels but is obviously much harder and less ethical to provide as you cannot instruct a carnivore on the most humane way of killing its prey. However, I have seen a Fishing cat exhibit that had a pond and stream in which live fish were kept. The cats would prowl up and down the edge of the water feature and occasionally leap with great enthusiasm into the water. There was usually a great splash and a flurry of activity worthy of a David Attenborough documentary. But fear not, the fish were seasoned campaigners and would slide away with barely a change in direction. Some of the cats gave up but others were not disheartened and continued stalking the fish vigilantly well into the night.

Street food

Dogs and ferrets love new flavours. Cats often prefer habit and familiarity. Then, of course, there are those individuals that break all the rules. Some cats will try anything.

Guinness was a dark brown, long-haired moggie who was found as a five-month-old kitten in a hawker's market-place in Singapore. She was a feisty little thing, used to fending for herself but also accustomed to demanding food from the humans living and working around her. A meal for her could be a tray of leftover chilli noodles, a piece of stingray, prawn heads, duck rice (recipe opposite) or even a half empty packet of potato chips. These eclectic tastes continued into her adult life. Despite being offered the highest quality pet food in her new home she was always on the lookout for something new and exciting.

Guinness also retained her street-fighting ways despite being adopted into a safe and comfortable home. She could not tolerate any new cat coming into her household. No matter how gradual the introduction, the poor newcomer would be chased out of the house in such a brutal way that it would not dare come back in. The only exception was a slow old chinchilla (very long, light blue/grey fur) called Ice. Ice wandered nonchalantly around his new house barely blinking as Guinness leapt upon him in a hissing fury. He never seemed to sustain any injuries. Guinness eventually gave up but was occasionally seen stalking around looking annoyed, with grey hair in her mouth and claws.

Fish nuggets

suitable for
cat, dog, ferret, turtle

preparation time
Short: 5–15 minutes to prepare and cook.

ingredients
200 g firm white fleshed fish fillets
1 egg
½ cup dry breadcrumbs
¼ cup plain flour
½ teaspoon salt
vegetable oil

method
Lightly beat the egg.
Mix the breadcrumbs, flour and salt.
Slice the fish into 2 cm cubes.
Dip each piece into the egg, and then roll in the breadcrumb mix.
Heat the vegetable oil in a frying pan over medium high heat.
Fry the fish pieces in batches until golden all over.

serve
Serve when cooled.

Salmon nuggets

This is an interesting variation on the fish nuggets recipe that uses salmon fat.

suitable for
cat, dog, ferret, turtle

preparation time
Medium: 15–45 minutes to prepare and cook.

ingredients
As listed for the fish nuggets but use the salmon fat mixed with vegetable oil to improve the flavour.

method
Cook some salmon for yourself for dinner. Then use the salmon fat and a little vegetable oil to fry the nuggets. The salmon fat gives a wonderful aroma and flavour to the nuggets which will entice most recovering cats to eat.

Chicken with anchovy and parmesan cream

This is decadence for both cats and dogs. It produces a very excited response whenever my pets smell the aroma of the combination of anchovies and fresh chicken. Beef Jerky, my 17-year-old black and white cat knows that if he waits patiently while I'm cooking he'll get a piece of raw chicken to bide his time while his dinner cools.

suitable for

cat, dog, ferret

preparation time

Medium: 15–45 minutes to prepare and cook.

ingredients

½ chicken fillet
60 g grated fresh parmesan
125 ml chicken stock (page 59)
1 tablespoon plain flour
1 tablespoon anchovy oil (page 98)

method

Cut the chicken fillet into 1 cm chunks.
Stir-fry over medium heat in a little of the anchovy oil. Cook until golden brown all over. Remove from pan.
Add the rest of the anchovy oil to pan and add flour off the flame. Stir till smooth with a wooden spoon.
Cook for 1–2 minutes. Gradually add the stock and stir constantly until boiling.
Reduce heat, add parmesan and cook for another 2 minutes.
Add sauce to chicken pieces.

serve

Serve when cooled.

Duck rice

suitable for

cat, dog, ferret

preparation time

Short: 5–15 minutes to prepare and cook.

ingredients

½ cup white rice
1 cup duck stock (page 112)
½ cup duck meat

method

Bring the stock and rice to the boil. Reduce to a simmer. Leave the lid on and allow the rice to cook by absorption for a further 12–14 minutes. This method should result in quite a wet rice and stock mix. If your cat prefers it drier, reduce the amount of stock to ¾ cup. Cool to room temperature.

serve

Serve 1 tablespoon of duck rice next to 1 tablespoon of duck meat.

Beverages

Cats like their water to be pristine and they can be very fussy about what sort of container they will drink from. Have you ever noticed that your cat prefers to drink from your glass on the table rather than his own water bowl? Cats depend heavily on their sense of smell for appetite. Water that is sitting next to the food bowl becomes tainted by the smell of that food. I find that cats also prefer to drink from a ceramic or glass bowl rather than plastic or stainless steel. Cats need plenty of drinking vessels and their water must always be spotlessly clean. They prefer it cool and certainly without lint or dust in it. It must be absolutely fresh!

Hydrangea is a great big male ginger cat who loves to get into fights, but he will only drink from the crystal bowl on his owner's kitchen window sill.

The weakest point of cats (and this includes some of the big cats, such as cheetahs) is often their kidneys. One of the most important factors in maintaining kidney health is a high level of water intake. This can be difficult with fussy cats (and that seems to apply to most cats I've met). Here are suggestions to increase your cat's water consumption.

Keep the water in a ceramic dish at least half a metre away from the food to prevent tainting. Place another glass or ceramic dish on the floor in the bathroom. Some cats like to be able to look down upon their domain as they drink so place another vessel up on a wide window ledge. Wash the vessels and change the water daily.

Fish stock

suitable for

cat, dog

preparation time

Long: over 45 minutes to prepare and cook.

ingredients

500 g fish bones and trimmings (I've found a Mediterranean supermarket which is great for these). Alternatively, you can use prawn heads (uncooked).
parsley
slice of lemon
2 cloves garlic
1 teaspoon salt

method

Add everything to a pot and add enough water to cover the bones with room to spare.
You will need to add a few cups extra if you use prawn heads.
Bring to the boil.
Reduce heat and simmer for half an hour.
Strain and store in the freezer.

Lassi

This drink is quite a treat for a cat that is partial to milk. Low-lactose milk is best. You can use cows', goats' or sheep's yoghurt. My cat is particularly partial to sheep's yoghurt. Sheep's yoghurt tastes deliciously creamy to me. Maybe it tastes that way to him too.

suitable for

cat, dog, ferret, rodent

preparation time

Short: 5–15 minutes to prepare.

ingredients

¼ cup low lactose milk
1 tablespoon natural unpasteurised yoghurt

method

Either use a blender to mix ingredients or shake well in a jar.

serve

Serve at room temperature.

The myth of milk

A classic picture from a child's storybook is that of the cat lapping from a bowl of milk. Whole milk is not a good food for most cats because it contains lactose. Lactose is usually the component that cats and dogs struggle to digest. A little is ok but a lot will result in diarrhoea. This can be avoided by feeding aged cheeses and unpasteurised yoghurt in which most of the lactose is hydrolysed. In some cases of diarrhoea, feeding natural unpasteurised yoghurt can even help restore normal intestinal order.

Party food, treats and snacks

Don't bother creating sweet treats for your cat as they are not often interested. Cats depend on fats and salts for palatability but these must be used in moderation of course. Textures are important too. The textures that your cat prefers, even including the shape of the dry food kibble, tend to be developed early in life and they become habit. Then of course there is scent. Wonderful aromas really get a cat's appetite going. They are not at all interested in the colour of their food, but we are so why not make it look nice too?

Mate's picnic

Mate is a cat that eats a raw, whole-food diet. If your cat has always been fed a wide variety of ingredients or is just plain adventurous, this picnic may appeal to him.

suitable for

cat, dog, lizard

preparation time

Short: 5–15 minutes to prepare.

ingredients

- 2 cubes raw beef steak
- ½ lamb fillet
- 1 chicken wing (raw and unseasoned)
- 1 roughly chopped mushroom
- sweet potato skin
- 1 slice roasted beetroot

serve

Feed ingredients separately as individual courses.

Beef's Christmas dinner

My 6-year-old son can't bear to see our cat Beef Jerky go without a special treat when we are all enjoying the decadence of Christmas dinner. So he ushered me to the market on Christmas morning and chose smoked salmon and yoghurt as special treats for Beef.

Beef was a very happy cat, and now both he and my son insist that he is given some whenever we have smoked salmon and scrambled eggs for breakfast.

suitable for

cat, dog, human

preparation time

Medium: 15–45 minutes to prepare and cook.

ingredients

- 4 slices smoked salmon
- 2 eggs
- 2 teaspoons yoghurt
- margarine

method

Beat the eggs and 1 teaspoon of yoghurt together until fluffy. Heat a frying pan and melt a little margarine in it. Pour in the eggs. Use a spatula to fold (not stir) the eggs while cooking. Remove from heat once cooked through but still moist.

Slice one of the smoked salmon pieces and leave the other three whole.

serve

Place the scrambled eggs and two pieces of smoked salmon on a plate for you.

Offer your cat one piece of smoked salmon sliced into 1 cm strips and one completely uncut. The shape of food often affects whether a cat is interested in it or not. Beef likes his cut up but other cats prefer to tackle it whole.

Put the remaining teaspoon of yoghurt and the salmon in separate dishes as most cats prefer these flavours separate.

caution

This is very salty so it should only be fed very occasionally.

Keeping the hunter at bay

One person's pet is another pet's dinner! One morning I had left my kitchen window open and came downstairs to find my neighbour's cat up to his elbows in my fish tank and with a mouthful of fish. I must say he knew quality when he saw it because they were very healthy fish and therefore a very well-balanced meal for him. I asked him politely not to come again!

When I worked at Singapore Zoo I had the unfortunate opportunity to examine many dead reticulated pythons. These pythons are native to Singapore but, like so many other places, there is often conflict between the humans and the snakes. Mostly, the pythons posed no threat to the humans as they preferred smaller prey like rats. On one occasion, we found something that in retrospect was surprisingly uncommon. The python's last meal had been a small dog wearing a pink collar. The python, of course, had not known the difference between acceptable wild and feral prey and someone's pet!

Cats try to eat budgies and dogs try to eat rabbits. We have some success training dogs in the etiquette of choosing what to eat but cats and pythons are reasonably recalcitrant where this is concerned.

We can ameliorate our cats' desire to hunt for their own prey by providing them with special treats. Creative treats for cats can be difficult to come by as they are strict carnivores and won't enjoy fruit or vegies.

Bee's moulded pork terrine

suitable for

cat, dog, ferret, lizard, turtle

preparation time

Long: over 45 minutes to prepare and cook.

ingredients

1 kg pork knuckles
2 litres water
2 cups rice
4 carrots, sliced
2 cups peas

method

Place bones and water in a large stock pot and bring to the boil. Reduce heat and continue cooking for another hour. Periodically skim the solids from the surface.
Strain out the bones and reserve the liquid stock.
Remove meat and chop.
Discard the bones.
Put the stock and meat back onto the stove and add rice.
Bring it back to the boil and cook for another 15 minutes.
Add carrots and peas. Simmer for 5 minutes.
Pour the liquid into small moulds such as muffin tins. Allow to cool on the bench top.
Refrigerate overnight.
Freeze in individual serves.

Bee's moulded fish terrine

suitable for

cat, dog, turtle

preparation time

Long: over 45 minutes to prepare and cook.

ingredients

1 kg fish bones
2 litres water
2 cups rice
4 parsnips, sliced
2 cups peas
15 g powdered gelatine

method

Place bones and water in a large stock pot and bring to the boil. Reduce heat and continue cooking for 30 minutes. Periodically skim the solids from the surface.
Strain out the bones and reserve the liquid stock.
Put the stock back onto the stove and add rice.
Bring it back to the boil and cook for another 15 minutes.
Add carrots and peas.
Cook for 5 minutes.
Add the gelatine and stir until dissolved.
Pour the liquid into small moulds such as muffin tins. Allow to cool on the bench top.
Refrigerate overnight.

tip

Some fish bones do not gelatinise as well as pork so you often need to add dissolved gelatine to the end-product before pouring it into the moulds.

Bee's moulded pork terrine

Cooking with cats

Cats are not often fond of crowds and strangers but they love to be included in family events. It seems a shame to always send them out of the kitchen when you are cooking and they are standing up against the cupboard begging. I agree that it's not in the best interests of hygiene to have them on the bench among your ingredients and tools, but how about inviting them to stay for a chat while you prepare something for both humans and animals alike? While you're cooking, put a few pieces of raw meat aside for them. Your cats can wind happily around your legs, and as long as you remember not to trip over them then everyone will be happy.

Visceral appetiser

The viscera are the internal organs of an animal. Blending a variety of organ meat is often a good appetite stimulant for cats when made into a paste and smeared onto the surface of other food. This is quite a fatty recipe so don't use it if your cat is prone to pancreatitis.

suitable for

cat, dog, ferret, turtle

preparation time

Short: 5–15 minutes to prepare and cook.

ingredients

1 chicken liver and lungs
¼ cup chopped whole raw fish (e.g. sardines or whitebait)
¼ cup beef liver
1 cow's or sheep's pancreas (if you can get it)
½ sheep kidney including the fat

method

Bring a pot of water to boil.
Add all ingredients and cook until no longer pink.
Allow to cool.
Chop finely.

serve

Serve only a tablespoon at a time.

tip

This may be made into a paste and smeared lightly onto roasted chicken or mixed with minced beef and dry-fried until browned.

Food as entertainment

How do you entertain a cat? They like to chase a ball of wool and your toes under the blankets. But what can you do for them while you are out? My old cat likes to sleep in front of the flickering television but what about those young active kittens out there? We talked about enrichment of animals in the chapter on dogs. Cats are excited by smells and by things that move, whether they are lions or leopards in the zoo or our little domestic companions. Try laying a scent trail and changing the scent from day-to-day. Find out what your cat most likes to play with and create a toy based on it.

Ranger, my neighbour's cat, likes to fish. However, he had no fish of his own so he used to watch mine through the window. He now has a special water bowl that has an insert in the bottom with a pretend seascape, including little fish figurines that move so he can chase them.

Fish agar cubes

suitable for
cat, dog, turtle

preparation time
Long: over 45 minutes to prepare and cook.

ingredients
2 cups fish stock (page 89)
75 g tinned tuna in spring water
4 teaspoons agar-agar powder

method
Heat the fish stock and agar-agar powder together.
Bring to the boil.
Stir frequently to encourage the agar-agar to dissolve.
Once the agar-agar has dissolved, add the tuna and mix thoroughly.
Allow to cool.
Pour onto a flat shallow tray to a depth of 1 cm.
Leave to set.
Cut agar-agar into cubes.

serve
Offer your cat a sample or two to become accustomed to them.
Fill a small heavy dish with water and add a few agar-agar treats. Watch your cat go fishing.

Dried liver treats

suitable for
cat, dog, ferret, turtle

preparation time
Long: over 45 minutes to prepare and cook.

ingredients
500 g liver (beef, chicken or pork)
2 crushed garlic cloves

method
Slice beef or pork liver into 2 cm slabs. Chicken livers are small enough to cook whole.
Drop liver and garlic into boiling water then reduce to simmer for about 20 minutes.
Remove the liver from the boiled water and allow it to cool until it can be handled.
Preheat the oven to 200 °C.
Slice liver into 1 cm strips and place on a greased baking tray.
Bake for 20–30 minutes.
This must be stored in the fridge in an airtight container once cooled.

tip
Both dried fish and dried liver make good treats to hide for your cat while you are out, as they don't go rancid quickly. Find an empty plastic mineral water bottle and place a handful of these treats inside. Show your cat how to push the bottle around to get the treats out.

Anchovy oil

This oil is useful to cook fish and vegetables for cats or to garnish fresh bones for animals that need a little encouraging.

suitable for

cat, dog, ferret, human

preparation time

Short: 5–15 minutes to prepare and cook.

ingredients

10 salted anchovy fillets, chopped finely
2 tablespoons olive oil

method

Heat the olive oil over low to medium heat.
Add the chopped anchovies and stir until they melt into the oil.

serve

Use when cooled as a relish for other dishes.

Cat pâté

suitable for

cat, dog, ferret, lizard

preparation time

Short: 5–15 minutes to prepare and cook.

ingredients

1 cup chopped beef liver
2 tablespoons bone marrow
½ garlic clove
1 tablespoon fresh catmint

method

Ask the butcher to cut open some large beef bones for you so that you can retrieve the marrow. Hopefully you also have a dog that you can offer the raw bones to! Alternatively, buy some osso bucco bones for yourself for dinner and sacrifice some of the marrow from one of the shanks. (There is a recipe for doggy osso bucco on page 14.)
Cook the chicken livers in boiling water until no longer pink.
Coarsely chop the chicken livers and combine with the rest of the ingredients.
Either blend the ingredients in a food processor or chop finely and then push through a sieve to refine.
Use an ice-cube tray to store these treats in the freezer.

serve

Make a treasure hunt for your cat. Defrost a cat pâté cube and smear some on a few garden leaves. Place them around the garden and in low branches of trees and let your cat find them. Remember where they all are because you will need to dispose of them on the same day if your cat doesn't find them, as they will decay.

Cats feeling poorly

Cats are amazing creatures. We often talk about how resilient they are. 'There goes another of his nine lives', we'll say as Tom misses his landing when leaping from the roof to the fence. But once a cat becomes ill and loses his appetite, it becomes much more critical to get him eating again, and quickly, than many other species.

Cats are prone to a condition called hepatic lipidosis when they go without food for prolonged periods or lose weight rapidly. Therefore, it is critical to get them eating again or to get them to hospital for assisted feeding if they haven't eaten anything for more than two days or if they seem to have lost a lot of weight quickly.

The most important factors in stimulating a cat's appetite are the smell and the temperature of the food. The two are also linked. By heating food slightly, the volatile aromas are released.

There are many conditions which can interfere with a cat's appetite. A blocked nose will impair her ability to smell the food. Ulcers in the mouth may damage taste buds and make eating painful. Dental and gum disease is painful and makes chewing a difficult task. Disease of the gastrointestinal system anywhere from the oesophagus to the anus can cause pain, blockages or poor digestion, all of which reduce appetite.

Some medications can have direct effects on the senses of smell and taste and can have other side effects that upset digestion.

Cats can also suffer dietary intolerances. Dairy intolerance is one that was mentioned earlier (page 89). High levels of fat can overcome the body's ability to digest it. Several jungle cats and clouded leopards under my care at Singapore Zoo were once afflicted with a dreadful foamy diarrhoea when the latest batch of lamb supplied was too fatty. Trimming most of the fat from the meat resolved the condition. I have also seen domestic cats that cannot tolerate particular types of meat. Some cats will develop diarrhoea with kangaroo meat. Others cannot tolerate beef. Meats that are rancid can cause vomiting or just general misery and inappetence. Toxins from raided compost bins can result in life-threatening illnesses.

There are many other special occasions for modifying a cat's diet. Some of them require very strict formulae and others merely require a short stint following particular guidelines. No matter whether your cat is sick or recovering from surgery, it is important that the building blocks needed for recovery are available. Sometimes you will be able to provide what your cat needs with the usual diet you have fed. On other occasions you may need to strictly adhere to a prescription diet. It is always worth asking your vet whether your cat can have any treats or home-prepared food to help nurse him back to health.

Treats for cats on restricted protein diets

These treats may be used for cats that need to have their protein intake restricted. They are not a complete diet. Please ask your vet if they are suitable to give as treats to your sick cat.

suitable for
cat

preparation time
Medium: 15–45 minutes to prepare and cook.

ingredients
- 60 g beef liver
- 60 g minced beef (premium, not diet mince)
- 1 egg
- 1 cup cooked rice (115 g)
- 4 tablespoons breadcrumbs
- ¼ teaspoon potassium chloride (diet salt)
- 1 tablespoon vegetable oil

method
Chop the beef liver until it resembles the mince. Mix with the mince, egg and cooked rice.

Mix the diet salt and breadcrumbs.

Form marble-sized meat balls and roll in the bread crumbs.

Gently fry in the vegetable oil until cooked through.

serve
Serve at room temperature.

Dry food meatballs

suitable for
cat

preparation time
Short: 5–15 minutes to prepare.

ingredients
- 500 g minced beef
- 2 cups dry cat food
- 1 egg
- ¼ cup wheat germ oil

method
Grind dry cat pellets in food processor or blender.

Mix all ingredients together, and then roll into balls.

Freeze individually then store together in freezer.

Defrost as needed.

One small step at a time

Mr Jones was a very uncomfortable and miserable cat. Everything made him cross. Nothing seemed to be good enough for him. He wouldn't eat anything offered to him, not even his favourite cut of steak. His owners couldn't work out what was wrong with him. The last straw was when Mr Jones started using their bed as a toilet. So off they all went to the vet. It turned out that Mr Jones had crystals forming in his urine and these were making it very difficult and painful to urinate. No wonder he was cross! Part of the treatment for Mr Jones was to be fed a highly specific prescription diet. Now most cats will turn their nose up at a new food in this situation, however they will accept it if it is introduced gradually over two weeks. The key is to only add a teaspoon of the new food on the first day. The amount of the new diet is increased incrementally each day as the amount of the old diet is decreased. Unfortunately, there can be no treats as cats are very good at training their owners to feed more treats and less prescription diet!

Mr Jones was particularly recalcitrant when it came to accepting the new food. 'Where is my steak?' you could almost hear him cry as he sifted through the dry food and carefully avoided eating the prescription diet. Together with the owner, we came up with this solution: crushed dry food with minced meat made into meat balls. This way we could gradually increase the amount of prescription diet and decrease the amount of mince. We gradually substituted the wet version of the diet and finally he would eat both the wet and dry prescription diet.

Affected by smell

Tinkerbell was only 5 weeks old and she had cat flu. She had sticky eyes and a runny nose and couldn't smell a thing. On top of that she had ulcers in her sore little mouth. Needless to say, she didn't feel much like eating. She had to be hospitalised, put on an intravenous drip to give her water and salt requirements, and had her leg bandaged to secure the drip. She was miserable. With no energy and no basic nutrients coming into her little body, no amount of medicine was going to help. We had to do something quickly. Her mouth was sore so we applied a baby teething gel to her ulcers. Her nose was blocked so we used a steam vaporiser to help clear it. She couldn't smell bland food so we found the fishiest, smelliest food we could and improved the aroma by mixing it with a little warm water. She finally took a sniff and started eating. Hooray!

Fish aromatherapy

suitable for
cat

preparation time
Short: 5–15 minutes to prepare and cook.

ingredients
1 tablespoon tinned tuna
1 tablespoon natural yoghurt

method
Heat the tuna for 5 seconds in the microwave on high.
Blend the tuna and the yoghurt.

serve
Serve lukewarm.

Weight-loss program for cats

He isn't fluffy he's just fat! Obesity is surprisingly common in cats and it is just as dangerous for cats as it is for other species. It puts greater stress on the heart and joints and makes cats more prone to cardiovascular and respiratory disease. Cats that have suffered from feline lower urinary tract disease will also be more likely to relapse if they are overweight. Overweight cats are less active and generally much less comfortable than their svelte friends.

It's Garfield's fault! I blame cartoon cats because they are often portrayed as being extra cute and cuddly when they are fat. It's important not to turn a blind eye to obesity in cats. How can you tell if your cat is overweight? If you can't feel his ribs or his hips and he doesn't have a waist line then he is overweight.

Weight loss in cats needs to be pursued carefully. Weigh your cat before you start and then continue weekly weigh-ins. Make an honest and complete diet chart over a week (as described in the dog chapter on page 69) and make an appointment to see the vet. If the veterinary examination rules out any disease, then you can begin the weight-loss program. This may involve changing to a different food or altering amounts of particular ingredients. Refer to 'Dogs feeling poorly' on page 52 for more detail.

Exercise is just as important for cats as it is for dogs. Unlike pet dogs, owners don't often take cats for walks. However, play time is a great form of exercise. Entice your cat to chase a piece of rolled-up paper for 10 minutes twice daily. Climb stairs and trees with him. Spread his food around the garden or the house and help him find it. Be inventive and get your cat moving!

Hairballs

Most cats are fastidious groomers and hairballs can be a problem, especially in those with long hair. A long-haired cat can regurgitate hair but sometimes the hair can cause constipation or gastric upsets. Both these conditions can benefit from dietary assistance. The signs in a cat are obvious when you step out of bed in the morning into a slimy lump of regurgitated hair! If this occurs often, your pet should be taken to the vet to rule out more sinister causes of vomiting.

There are plenty of preparations available for cats to assist in the movement of hair through the gastrointestinal tract and out the other end. They usually come in paste form with specific instructions. There are also commercial diets available that address the problem in cats.

A well-balanced diet will help prevent skin disease and ensure strong skin and fur. Good diet, in combination with brushing them daily will help reduce the occurrence of gastric furballs.

Food that cats should avoid

Chocolate

Chocolate is highly toxic to cats.

The most common times of year for the Lort Smith Animal Hospital to be presented with animals suffering from chocolate toxicity are Easter and Christmas. The brightly glittering foil wrapped eggs and other goodies sparkling in the moonlight can make exciting toys for cats and they soon discover they are edible. The toxic compound in chocolate causes nervous system excitement which may even lead to seizures, cardiac arrhythmias and death.

Do not allow your cat to eat any chocolate.

Onions, leek, garlic, chives

Cats are extremely sensitive to onion toxicity so it is best to avoid feeding them onions in any quantity. Onions cause a particular type of anaemia due to damage to the red blood cells of cats.

The following shows how little onion is required to cause illness. The toxic dose can be as low as 5 g/kg onions in cats. A 3 kg cat would need 15 g onions to be affected. However, to be safe I would not include any in your pet recipes.

Leek, chives and garlic can also be toxic but only in much larger amounts. Some of our pet recipes include garlic at safe levels.

Mushrooms

Do not feed your cat wild mushrooms. There are many possible toxic effects and it is difficult to identify which mushrooms are safe.

ferrets

what do ferrets need?

110
Meals

114
Beverages

114
Party food, treats and snacks

115
Food as entertainment

120
Ferrets feeling poorly

124
Food that ferrets should avoid

Ferrets are true carnivores as are cats, and do very well on a diet similar to cats. It is imperative that they are offered animal products (muscle meat, organ meat, bone) as their bodies cannot make do with a vegetarian diet.

Ferrets do well when fed commercial cat food diets. They can also be fed a fresh, home-cooked, meat-based diet, but like any other carnivore, this needs to be balanced with added vitamins, minerals, oils and fibres.

Ferrets are easier to supplement than cats because their curiosity seems to lead to better acceptance of new ingredients in their diet. They also love to chew things!

Beware of changing your ferret to a whole-food diet if they aren't used to it. One of my patients was given a whole duckling as a treat. Having no experience with whole prey he ate the lot, beak and all, without much chewing. He had to have surgery to remove the beak and a bunch of feathers from his intestine as it had caused a blockage. He recovered well but is now eating his cat food again.

Meals

A diet based on the cat diet but with a few extras to satisfy their curiosity should work well for your ferret. They need high protein levels and moderate levels of fat in their diet. Being true carnivores, there are some nutrients they can only obtain from animal sources. A ferret cannot survive on a vegetarian diet, nor can they survive eating muscle alone. They are quite adventurous in their tastes if introduced to a wide range of ingredients as kits. Don't be afraid to try new ingredients or recipes. Ferrets often like new flavours and textures and don't seem to be as prone to forming dietary habits as cats. However, they do seem to enjoy sweet things and this is not healthy for them if too much is included in their diet.

Beef, chicken and vegetables

suitable for
ferret, dog, cat

preparation time
Medium: 15–45 minutes to prepare and cook.

ingredients
1 chicken wing
100 g fresh beef
1 fresh chicken liver
¼ carrot
¼ apple
1 brussel sprout
4 spinach leaves
½ teaspoon vegetable oil

method
Offer your ferret the raw chicken wing as an appetiser.
Finely chop the beef and liver.
Fry the beef and liver gently in the oil until thoroughly browned.
Juice the carrot and the apple. Keep both the pulp and the juice.
Finely chop the brussels sprout and the spinach leaves.
Mix the beef, chicken liver, apple and vegetables together thoroughly.

serve
Serve at room temperature.

tip
This mix may be frozen in portions.

Casserole of roasted duck

suitable for
ferret, dog, cat

preparation time
Long: over 45 minutes to prepare and cook.

ingredients
1 whole roasted duck
1 tablespoon salt
1 carrot
1 capsicum
1 parsnip

method
Slice the vegetables finely.
Cut the duck into quarters. Remove the oil gland and the tail and discard.
Place the duck and vegetables into a large pot and fill with water so that the meat is fully immersed.
Bring to the boil, and then simmer for 1 hour. Periodically skim fat from the surface.
When the duck starts to fall off the bone, the casserole is ready.
Remove the bones and skin carefully from the pot and discard.
Allow the casserole to cool while stirring to break up the duck meat.

serve
There are several options for serving.
Serve as a casserole at room temperature.
Strain the solids and serve those as a meal, reserving the liquid.
Make an agar treat with the stock (page 116).

Beverages

Ferrets will happily drink from and play in water from a dish. It is important that the vessel be easy to clean and easy to fill. Lucy the ferret loves to roll around in her water. Many ferrets love to play in water so it is a good idea to have several sources so that they always have a full clean dish to drink from somewhere. A deep baking tray provides a good play pool for ferrets.

Party food, treats and snacks

I think young ferrets are like little boys. Why sit still when there are people to see, places to go and exciting objects to find that you really shouldn't play with but just can't resist? And they love a party! How could we say no to them? There are so many types of food that ferrets like it is not hard to find them a treat, especially if they are trained to eat a variety of ingredients from an early age. Don't be afraid to experiment but remember that treats are only special if they are given occasionally. If you give them too often they are no longer exciting and they can interfere with a balanced diet.

Food as entertainment

Ferrets are naturally good at entertaining themselves and will find all sorts of adventures to go on if left to their own devices. This isn't always the safest thing to do so you have to provide them with their own little safe haven (also known as a cage!) when you go out. This is where enrichment devices and techniques come in. Just like meerkats at the zoo, ferrets love to explore.

Duck and grape agar-agar

suitable for
ferret, dog, lizard, turtle

preparation time
Long: over 45 minutes to prepare and cook.

ingredients
500 ml cold duck stock (page 112).
2 teaspoons agar-agar powder (agar-agar is used to make some Asian desserts. It is similar to gelatine but results in a firmer finish. You can find it in some Asian grocers.)
10 mint leaves
2 grapes

method
Pour the stock into a pot and add the agar-agar powder. Gradually bring to the boil while stirring continuously until the agar-agar dissolves completely.
Remove from heat and pour into an oven tray.
Allow it to set.
Cut into ferret bite-sized cubes.
Tear up the mint leaves.
Quarter the grapes.

serve
Add the grapes and the mint leaves to the agar-agar cubes.

tip
The agar-agar cubes should be stored in an airtight container in the fridge without the mint and the grapes if you aren't going to use it all.

Beef aspic

suitable for
ferret, dog, cat, lizard, turtle

preparation time
Long: over 45 minutes to prepare and cook.

ingredients
dried fish
500 g beef knuckles
1 litre water
1 cup rice
2 carrots, sliced
1 cup peas

method
Place bones and water in large stock pot and bring to the boil. Reduce heat and continue cooking for another hour. Skim the solids from the surface periodically.
Strain out the bones and reserve the liquid.
Put the stock back onto the stove and add rice.
Bring it back to the boil and cook for another 15 minutes.
Add carrots and peas. Simmer for 5 minutes.
Pour the liquid into small moulds such as muffin tins. Allow to cool on the bench top.
Refrigerate overnight.

serve
Serve at room temperature.

Liver brownies

suitable for
ferret, dog, cat, turtle

preparation time
Long: over 45 minutes to prepare and cook.

ingredients
500 g beef or pork liver
1 cup plain flour
½ cup polenta
1 crushed garlic clove

method
Preheat oven to 180 °C.
Blend all ingredients in a food processor until they form a smooth paste.
Grease a flat baking tray and line with baking paper.
Bake for 20 minutes or until browned all over.

serve
Serve when cool.

Liver brownies

Yoghurt icy poles

suitable for
ferret, dog, cat, rodent, human

preparation time
Long: over 45 minutes to prepare.

ingredients
½ cup natural yoghurt (unpasteurised)

method
Beat the yoghurt with a fork until it is smooth.
Spoon into ice-cube trays or dollop onto foil on a flat plate.
Put them in the freezer overnight.
The next day the icy poles can be removed from their container or tray and stored in a plastic bag together in the freezer.

serve
Serve frozen.

Bacon and quail egg salad

suitable for
ferret, dog, cat, human

preparation time
Short: 5–15minutes to prepare and cook.
This is a great picnic dish for ferrets.

ingredients
4 quail eggs (fresh from the market or cooked from the delicatessen)
1 piece of bacon

method
Bring a pot of water to the boil.
Meanwhile cut the bacon into bite-sized squares and fry. Drain on a piece of kitchen towel.
Add the quail eggs to the water when boiling. Boil for 3 minutes.
Allow ingredients to cool. Remove the shell from the eggs.

serve
Put it all in an airtight container and off you go on your picnic!

Ferrets feeling poorly

Ferrets are quite prone to respiratory infections and inflammation. A ferret with a runny nose doesn't tend to feel too poorly but can be quite noisy with all the snuffling and throat clearing. Sometimes they also end up with a fever or even a deeper chest infection and this is when they start to be miserable. Once they've been off to the vet and been given their medicine it doesn't hurt to molly coddle them a little.

Turn on the shower to create some steam. Bring your ferret into the bathroom on their favourite jumper of yours. Ferrets are highly aware of scents. As well as making good use of their own strong scent they are very attached to the scent of their owners. They will feel much safer when they are able to burrow deep into a jumper or T-shirt of yours rather than a brand new blanket bought especially for them. Once you've settled her into the bathroom, go and get some of her favourite food. As her head clears she will become more enthusiastic about eating. Try a piece of roast chicken or a little tinned tuna. Perhaps a little honey on a piece of sausage. Something not too rough or hard is likely to be the most appealing to a ferret with a sore throat. You could even try making some mint tea and adding a little honey and cold water. Honey is great for sore throats.

The Blu Tack incident

Lucy the ferret was one such curious ferret. In other words, she was into everything. One evening she was presented to me in a terribly subdued state. She wasn't eating or going to the toilet. An X-ray showed nothing. The following day she was no better and was sick enough to make us very worried. We took her into theatre for an exploratory surgery. Sure enough, a foreign object was found to be blocking her small intestine. It was a piece of Blu Tack. The only Blu Tack that the owner had was on her desk and was thought to be quite out of reach.

Let that be a lesson. Beware the investigating ferret wandering free at night. You never know what they might find and eat!

Mint tea jelly

suitable for
ferret, bird, rodent

preparation time
Long: over 45 minutes to prepare and cook.

ingredients
1 cup freshly cut mint leaves
2 cups boiling water
2 teaspoon agar-agar powder

method
Boil the kettle.
Wash the mint leaves.
Pour the boiling water over the mint and cover.
Allow it to cool to room temperature.
Add the agar-agar powder and bring the water back to the boil. Stir constantly until the agar-agar dissolves.
Pour into ice-cube moulds once cooled.

serve
Serve on a hot day.

Duck soup

suitable for
ferret, dog, cat

preparation time
Long: over 45 minutes to prepare and cook.

ingredients
As listed for the roasted duck casserole recipe (page 112).

method
Make the stock as described in roasted duck casserole recipe.
Strain the solids.

serve
Serve the stock cool as soup.

Dental surgery recovery diet

I've found that big pieces of firm meat are the best thing to feed to carnivorous mammals after dental extractions. Soft pasty or mushy food has a greater chance of lodging in the cavity left behind in the gums, which will result in pain and possibly infection.

suitable for

ferret, dog, cat

preparation time

Short: 5–15 minutes to prepare and cook.

ingredients

- 50 g beef fillet
- 50 g lamb fillet
- olive oil

method

Cut the beef and the lamb into 1 cm chunks. You will need about 1 tablespoon of each.

Fry them in the olive oil until golden brown and aromatic.

serve

Feed when cool.

Snowy's battle

I have a very sad story to tell about a ferret that had been fed only chicken muscle meat all his life. His name was Snowy. He was presented to me in a condition so weak that he could barely move. His owner had brought Snowy in because he had lost his appetite and kept dropping his food. When I opened his mouth to examine his teeth I found plaque thicker than all of his teeth. His teeth had shown amazing resilience not to fall out but they were no longer visible. His mouth smelled terrible and the gums were terribly infected. The diet of chicken meat lacked most vitamins and had next to no calcium. There was no fibre and no carbohydrate. This had resulted in a very weak body that could not build or repair any tissues, let alone fight infection. We started medical and supportive treatment for him as he was too weak to face surgery, but unfortunately it was too late. He died the next day.

Snowy's case is an extreme example of what can go wrong when unbalanced diets are fed. Many ferrets, cats and dogs will develop dental disease in their lifetime despite being fed a relatively well-balanced diet. Dental treatment requires an anaesthetic in animals as they will not stay still with their mouths open while their teeth are scaled. In a normal situation, the animal's underlying health is good and there is very little risk associated with the procedure even when extractions are required.

Food that ferrets should avoid

Chocolate

Chocolate can cause damage to the red blood cells of some mammals. The toxic dose for ferrets has not been studied. It is best not to feed any chocolate at all to your ferret.

Onions

Onions also have toxic effects on dogs and cats and it is possible that they could have the same effect on ferrets. As such they are best avoided.

Ferrets and foreign bodies

In the veterinary profession the term 'foreign body' is used to describe an object that is lodged somewhere it shouldn't be within the body.

There is something very important to note with ferrets: they have a tendency to explore the world with their mouths! They have been known to eat all sorts of things that they shouldn't.

birds

what do birds need?

128
Meals

134
Beverages

137
Party food, treats and snacks

140
Food as entertainment

146
Birds feeling poorly

149
Food that birds should avoid

Birds have the greatest variety of digestive systems, lifestyles and body shapes and sizes of all the pets we will try to pamper in this book. Large parrots such as cockatoos and galahs, as well as small parrots like budgies, eat a variety of seeds, leaves, grasses, flowers and native fruits in the wild. Rainbow lorikeets eat a mostly nectar-based diet. Owls and eagles hunt for prey such as rats and mice, bats, wallabies and rabbits. Tawny frogmouths eat a lot of moths. Fruit doves eat mostly fruit and hardly need to drink as the fruit is so moist. Flamingos are filter feeders. Penguins and seagulls eat fish. Even that list doesn't include all the categories.

The birds I have included here are those we see most commonly as pets brought into the Lort Smith Animal Hospital. Parrots, chickens and ducks will be emphasised but I won't be able to resist telling you tales of some other beautiful birds.

So how do you decide what to feed your bird? 'What does it need?' is the question to ask before 'What does it like?' Birds, like humans, don't necessarily have enough nutritional wisdom to eat a balanced diet from a wide choice of ingredients. They are quite likely to choose the ingredients they like most and avoid the rest.

Parrots have an interesting way of treating their food to make it easier to eat. We often cook our food to do the same thing. Many birds have a crop, which is a little pouch at the top of the chest that the oesophagus empties into. Seed-eating parrots such as cockatoos, galahs, corellas, budgies and cockatiels store their seed in their crops to warm and soak it. This makes the seed easier to digest when it then empties into the gizzard (bird stomach). The gizzard is a very thick-walled, hard stomach with grit inside it. It grinds the food down. This process is a little like making breakfast cereal where the grain is steamed and then rolled to make it easy for us to digest.

Galahs, *cockatoos*, *budgies* and *cockatiels* may love seed but they need to be trained early on to eat other ingredients that replace the leaves, flowers, grasses and various other ingredients that wild birds also eat. We tend to use a mixture of chopped vegetables and leafy greens as well as some form of calcium supply (either in pelleted form or cuttlefish bone).

Chickens eat quite a varied diet. They do very well on a combination of seeds and grains if they also have free access to your garden where they can forage for shoots, buds and insects to complete their diet. If they don't have access to a garden they will need to be either fed a complete pellet diet or be supplemented with green and orange vegetables, a protein and a calcium source along with their seed and grain mix.

Ducks often spend time foraging for food both on land and in the water. On land they look for seeds and grain and in the water they dive for fish, invertebrates, and water plants. They will eat grass, snails, grains and a variety of chopped vegetables when kept as pets.

Oatmeal and broccoli biscuits (page 138)

Meals

Birds, like any other pet, need a balanced diet and each species has different requirements. Chickens, for instance, require much higher levels of dietary calcium than cockatiels, even when they are not laying.

A common reason for birds being presented to vet clinics is egg-binding. Bubbles the cockatiel, had been looking like she was having trouble passing her droppings. She spent most of her time straining away on the edge of her perch rather than eating or talking. When she was examined by her vet it was discovered that she was trying to lay an egg. Part of her treatment involved an injection of calcium. The owner wondered why Bubbles needed more calcium when the egg that was stuck and the ones passed previously in the same clutch seemed perfectly formed with good hard shells. Bubbles didn't have a mate at home but had been a prolific egg-layer. As there was nothing physical blocking the passage of the egg, it was likely that her little body had started to run out of reserves as it continued to build solid eggs. Her poor little bones and muscles were becoming weaker and her oviduct was so worn out that it could no longer pass the egg.

Diets based solely on seed are common culprits for causing nutritional diseases. Birds may become obese when they choose to eat mostly high fat seeds like sunflowers and peanuts. The high levels of fats can end up causing deficiencies of other nutrients. All-seed diets don't have enough calcium or protein. Seed diets must always be supplemented with other ingredients that balance their inherent deficiencies.

Cage furniture

Bobby the budgerigar had me well-trained. Whenever he tired of his native timber perches he would toss them out of his cage. No matter how well-anchored they were, he would work them loose and eventually heave them out, even if it took him all day. This was his signal to me to go out and cut some new perches. So, off I'd go to find some interesting new bottle-brush twigs with the flowers, eucalypt branches with the nuts or occasionally even some grevillea. I'd always make sure I chose plants well away from the road and avoided places where insecticides or weed killers may have been sprayed. Before renovating his cage I would wash the branches under the shower for several minutes to remove any obvious contamination from other animals.

Parrots that are native to Australia love to feed on native plants. They usually prefer plants that are native to or similar to those found in their species' natural habitat. They will nibble leaves, flowers, nuts and bark. They'll give their beaks and nails a manicure on the rough surfaces. There are all sorts of exciting things to be found under the bark and inside the nuts. Natural perches can provide hours of entertainment, even when their nutritional value has declined and they've dried out (refer to Bush tucker recipe on page 141).

Mixed seed platter

Galahs, cockatiels and ring-necked parrots love this dish.
The oats in this dish are a good source of protein. The seeds are good for energy and vitamin E. The spinach contains a variety of other vitamins and minerals. Broccoli has good levels of calcium for a vegetable. Cuttlefish bone is an excellent source of calcium but not all birds will eat it.

suitable for

bird

preparation time

Short: 5–15 minutes to prepare.

ingredients

- 2 teaspoons canary seed
- 5 teaspoons mixed millet seeds
- 1 teaspoon hulled oats
- 2 teaspoons grey sunflower seeds
- ½ teaspoon finely chopped raw broccoli

method

Mix the seeds together on a platter.

Steamed vegetables

suitable for

bird, dog, lizard, rodent

preparation time

Short: 5–15 minutes to prepare and cook.

ingredients

- 1 broccoli floret
- 1 cauliflower floret
- 1 capsicum strip 1 cm wide
- ½ a brussel sprout

method

Steam the vegetables.
Steam larger amounts of each than mentioned in this recipe and use them for your own dinner. Keep a little of each for your parrot, duck or chicken.

serve

For small birds, such as budgies and cockatiels, you can offer a single piece of a different type of vegetable each day. Offer them steamed or just raw. You can also chop the steamed vegies, grate them or mash them into a pulp and make biscuits (only for a special treat!)

tip

Spend time with your bird when introducing a new ingredient. Play with the food with them. Pretend to eat it yourself. If they don't eat it at first, don't give up. Sometimes it takes several weeks of exploration and exposure before a bird will eat something new.

Mixed seed platter

Bobby's salad

For the ingredients of this recipe I'm sending you outside on a search-and-discover mission. If you have a garden with herbs and grass then you needn't go far. If not, then all is not lost. Keep on walking via your local park, pick the clover and continue on to the market or the greengrocer.

suitable for

bird, rabbit, guinea pig, rodent

preparation time

Short: 5–15 minutes to prepare.

ingredients

1 small handful of fresh picked clover (about ¼ cup)
3 parsley stalks with leaves
2 mint stalks with leaves
1 celery head (just the leaves from the top of one celery stick)

method

Wash the freshly picked clover and herbs under running water in a sieve or tea strainer in the sink.
Tear up all of the leaves; don't cut them as they lose too much of their natural texture and often the juices as well.
Mix the leaves with the clover and serve.

Sprouted seed salad

Parrots of any size will like this salad and benefit greatly from the change in nutrients in the seeds as they sprout. Use a budgie or cockatiel seed mix that doesn't have any grit, vitamin supplements or other additives. Make sure they are fresh seeds and clean. Hygiene is extremely important when sprouting seeds as they remain warm and moist for several days, providing excellent conditions for bacterial and fungal growth.

suitable for

bird, guinea pig, rodent

preparation time

Long: over 45 minutes to prepare.

ingredients

1 teaspoon budgie small seed mix
1 teaspoon wheat
¼ teaspoon sunflower seeds
¼ teaspoon mung beans

method

Rinse seeds thoroughly under running water.
Place seed mix in a small container and cover with household bleach diluted to 10% (that means 100 ml bleach to 900 ml water).
Soak the seed overnight in this solution.
Thoroughly wash and disinfect any equipment you will use. This includes your hands!
Rinse the soaked seed thoroughly for 2 minutes in a strainer in the sink.
Place the soaked seed into seedling trays to a maximum depth of 2 cm. Alternatively, you could use a flat tray covered with a couple of layers of wet kitchen paper towel.
Place in a warm place such as a window ledge that receives plenty of sun all day (more shelter may be needed in summer).
Check moisture levels in the trays twice daily. If they are drying out pour some water gently along the base of the sprouts, not on top of them as this is more likely to result in mouldy sprouts. Mould can be recognised by black spots, grey filaments and mouldy odour. If any of these are present, discard the whole batch.
When sprouted, remove from seed trays, rinse well and place in refrigerator.

Green salad

suitable for
bird, rabbit, guinea pig, rodent

preparation time
Short: 5–15 minutes to prepare.

ingredients
1 cup watercress
1 cup dandelion greens
½ cup spinach
½ cup sliced green beans

method
Offer all the ingredients rinsed and whole, or tear up the leaves and slice the beans if your chicken, duck or parrot prefers smaller pieces.

Green salad for ducks

suitable for
bird

preparation time
Short: 5–15 minutes to prepare.

ingredients
½ cup chickweed
½ cup silverbeet
½ cup endive
½ cup dandelion
½ cup duckweed

method
Offer all the ingredients rinsed and whole, or tear up if your duck prefers smaller pieces.

Green salad for parrots

suitable for
bird

preparation time
Short: 5–15 minutes to prepare.

ingredients
sow thistle (*Sorghum*)
sprouted millet
winter grass (*Poa annua*)
chickweed (*Certastium glomeratum*)
spinach
endive
dandelion

method
Offer all the ingredients rinsed and whole, or tear up if your parrot prefers smaller pieces.

Crop complaints

Henrietta, the Rhode Island Red hen, had to be kept indoors while she recovered from a digestive upset. She'd had trouble with a blocked crop that caused her to regurgitate her food. The crop is a wide part of the oesophagus where food is stored and moistened for a few hours after it is swallowed and before it reaches the gizzard (bird stomach). A short stay in hospital allowed us to diagnose and treat her problem. We suspected that Henrietta had eaten something that had disagreed with her. It may have been some grain that had been left out in the garden too long and had become mouldy. She needed plenty of fluids for her crop to be flushed out so that she could start afresh. Henrietta was a delightful patient. She would perch on our hands like a budgie whenever we took her out of her hospital cage and took her medications without complaint.

When she went home she needed to stay inside to keep warm and safe while she recovered her strength. That meant no more browsing in the owner's vegetable and herb garden for a while. The owners had to do the picking for her. Adjacent is a list of ingredients that Henrietta was fed in addition to her mixed grains and seeds.

Beverages

Water is the most essential ingredient in the diet. It must be provided in containers that are easy to clean and are easy for your birds to access. The water containers need to be placed in positions that minimise the potential for faecal contamination. Parrots are climbing and perching birds, as are some ducks. Water dishes should not be placed under areas where birds might perch. If you have many birds in one enclosure then you will need to provide many watering stations.

Birds also like to play in water, not just ducks, but parrots too. Rainbow lorikeets especially love to do this. Provide your bird with a big dish filled with a few centimetres of water only.

A bird fed an excessive level of protein is likely to end up with kidney failure. Animal products are usually high in protein. Vegetables high in protein include pulses such as lentils and peas. This is not a common problem. The more common cause of kidney problems is insufficient water intake due to contamination or inadequate supply.

Encourage your parrot's water intake by making a herbal infusion from fresh sage, chamomile, dandelion, licorice root or cloves.

Lorikeet love

A little lorikeet that had fallen or crashed when learning to fly, came into my care. He recovered quickly but had to stay in a cage by himself until his adult feathers were completely grown and he could safely try flying again. Each day, we placed a dish of water in the bottom of the cage but he ignored it, until one day, another lorikeet came in and all of a sudden the first chick was splashing and singing in the water at the top of his voice. I could swear he was inviting the other bird to play. We put them together and it was love at first sight. After a short time they were both well enough and fit enough to be released together. What a rewarding sight!

Herbal tea

If your parrot is a little out of sorts or even if you want to give her a special treat, try making her some herbal tea.

suitable for

bird, rodent, human

preparation time

Short: 5–15 minutes to prepare.

ingredients

- sage
- chamomile
- dandelion
- licorice root
- clove

method

Make the tea.

serve

Allow it to cool.

caution

Do not add any milk or sugar!
Never give caffeinated tea to birds.

Party food, treats and snacks

Saffron the lupin budgie loved to sit on his owner's shoulder and have just a little of her sweet biscuit when she was having a cup of tea. The problem was that a little bit to a person can be an awful lot to a tiny bird like a budgie. It is very soothing and satisfying to share your food with your bird and there is no reason that they should not enjoy special food treats. In fact I often find myself discussing recipes and treat ideas with my bird clients. Whether you own a chicken, a duck, a canary or a cockatoo, you will know your bird's favourite treats. Just remember to keep these in proportion within a balanced diet and keep your bird happy on the inside as well as the outside. Then feel free to experiment. You will find plenty of other bird owners who like to do the same.

Natural seed bells

suitable for

bird, rodent

preparation time

Medium: 15–45 minutes to prepare.

ingredients

20 gumnuts
2 tablespoon honey
1 tablespoon apple juice
¼ cup millet seeds

method

Collect fresh or dried gumnuts. Wash and dry them well in the sun.
Warm the honey and apple juice together briefly in the microwave. Mix well.
Using a basting brush, paint the inside of the gumnuts with honey or dip the entire gumnut in the honey mix.
Sprinkle the seeds over and inside the nut.

serve

Best served fresh.

tip

For a variation on this reciepe replace the apple juice with ¼ teaspoon of sesame oil and replace the millet seeds with sesame seeds.

Oatmeal and broccoli biscuits

suitable for

bird, dog, rodent

preparation time

Medium: 15–45 minutes to prepare and cook.

ingredients

70 g plain flour
40 g almond meal
85 g oatmeal
½ teaspoon baking powder
1 egg
85 g steamed, mashed broccoli

method

Preheat oven to 180 °C.
Mix the broccoli and flour.
Beat the egg.
Mix all ingredients together and knead into a stiff dough.
Place it in the freezer for about 20 minutes.
Separate the mix into marble-sized balls of dough and place on an oiled oven tray.
Bake 10–15 minutes.

Seed sticks

suitable for

bird, guinea pig, rodent

preparation time

Medium: 15–45 minutes to prepare.
These treats can be hung in cages and are reasonably healthy as well as being entertaining for your bird.

ingredients

10 apple or apricot tree twigs (forked twigs are easier to hang)
1 cup small seed mix
1 teaspoon dried fruit finely diced
¼ teaspoon crushed cuttlefish bone
4 egg whites
Breadcrumbs
1 tablespoon honey

method

Wash and dry the twigs.
Preheat the oven to 180 °C. Place twigs inside while it heats to dry them out.
Beat the eggs whites until fluffy but not stiff.
Mix with the seed, dried fruit and crushed cuttlefish.
Gradually add breadcrumbs until the mixture becomes sticky rather than wet.
Remove the sticks from the oven and press the mixture onto them.
Bake on an ungreased oven tray for 30 minutes or until firm and golden.
Remove from the oven and baste with honey.
Turn off the heat and allow the seed sticks to dry inside while it cools.

Natural seed bells

Food as entertainment

New scents and flavours are fascinating to birds. They can also be used to keep them busy while the rest of their flock is out at work or school. In zoos, we use scents as a form of enrichment or entertainment for the animals. Here I have adapted some of the techniques we used to be suitable for parrots.

Parrots love to explore and dismantle anything they can get their beaks on. Instead of buying them new plastic toys or mirrors, think about the sorts of things wild parrots play with. Put a eucalypt branch with the bark still on it in the bottom of the cage. Hide some seeds inside a dried bottle brush flower, or better still, put the whole branch in—including fresh leaves and flowers.

Vase of fresh leaves

For birds it is exciting to have fresh leaves, freshly washed and dripping dew-like droplets.

suitable for

bird

preparation time

Short: 5–15 minutes to prepare.

ingredients

fresh native leaves such as *Grevillea*, *Banksia*, gum, bottlebrush

method

Pick the leaves and wash, leaving some water droplets on them.

Place in a vase.

tip

Leaves keep fresh for up to 3 days.

Bush tucker for Australian native birds

suitable for

bird

preparation time

Short: 5–15 minutes to prepare.

ingredients

leaves, seeds, nuts and flowers of the following plants: wattle trees (*Acacia*), eucalypts, *Grevillea*, *Banksia*, bottlebrush, *Hakea*, *Melaleuca*, *Casuarina*

handful of native grasses with or without seed and flower heads.

Insects such as wood-boring larvae.

method

Pick the leaves, seeds, nuts and flowers.

Pick the grasses.

Peel back the bark on trees to look for the insects.

Wash what you've picked under running water. (I use the shower for my gum branches.)

serve

Place into your bird's cage as a perch. Alternatively, you can take your bird out and pretend to share the leaves and flowers with her. Pet birds often see you as a member of their flock and are greatly encouraged to eat something new if they see you eating it first.

tip

Choose plants that don't have high levels of human or motor traffic over or near them to reduce contamination by feet, oils and exhaust fumes.

Australian grass seeds

One way you can liven up the diet of your seed-eating bird is to sprout the seeds that they would eat if they were wild birds living in their natural habitat. Do a bit of research for your bird and find out the species names of some of the seeds it eats in the wild.

Wild budgerigars eat a wide variety of seeds. Try asking your local nursery if they have these seeds or plants and follow their instructions to try sprouting them:

- Weeping grass (*Microlaena stipoides*)
- Wallaby grass (*Austrodanthonia* species)
- Kangaroo grass (*Themeda triandra*)
- Redgrass (*Bothrichia macra*)
- Native millet (*Panicum decompositum*)
- Barley Mitchell grass (*Astrelba pectinata*)
- Spinifex (*Trioda*)
- Button grass (*Dactylocterium radulans*)

Tussie mussie (page 144)

Tussie mussie

Tussie mussie is what my mum calls a posy of herbs picked from the garden. My cat loves to rub up against it especially if it contains rosemary sprigs. I also discovered that budgies like it.

Patients often end up coming home with me! They often need that extra care you can't give in the hospital and when they are strays they have no owners to give it to them. Bobby the budgie was brought into the clinic by a client in terrible distress. Her cat had caught him and brought him home to her. Bobby had terrible wounds, which we repaired, but he just wouldn't start eating for himself again. We could not find his owner and the lady who brought him in loved her cat and felt she couldn't safely keep Bobby. My concern was that he was just too stressed in the hospital environment to make a complete recovery. So I took him home for a bit of TLC and he became our pet.

I set him up with the usual budgie seed, supplement and vegie mix, but what really seemed to do the trick was a bit of aromatherapy. I pegged one of my mum's tussie mussies to the cage next to his perch and gave him a eucalyptus perch instead of the old dowel. He immediately started nibbling at the herb leaves and then preening himself.

His appetite has been great from that point onwards.

Rosemary scented oil

suitable for
bird, human

preparation time
Long: over 45 minutes to prepare.

ingredients
- 2 cups olive oil
- 4 sprigs rosemary
- sealable glass jar or bottle

method
Wash the rosemary and pat dry with paper towel.

Put the rosemary into the bottle. Make sure the rosemary is completely covered by oil.

Pour the oil over it.

Allow it to steep for 2 weeks.

tip
Use it like the adjacent scented oils recipe or in your own cooking.

Tussie mussie

suitable for
bird

preparation time
Short: 5–15 minutes to prepare.

ingredients
- 4 basil leaves
- 2 sprigs rosemary
- 6 sage leaves (one sprig with the smaller leaves)
- 4 mint leaves

method
Pick the herbs fresh from the garden or buy them.

Put together in a posy and place inside your bird's cage.

Provide a container of fresh water broad enough for your bird to bathe in near the herbs.

caution
Place the posies within the twigs of a branch; don't tie them just in case your budgie eats the string or elastic band.

Birds feeling poorly

Birds have a very rapid metabolism compared to most mammals. This means that they have high energy needs even when they are relatively inactive. With the exception of the fish-eaters and birds of prey, most birds need to eat frequently throughout the day. This becomes especially important when they are sick or injured. And yet this is the time when they have the least desire to eat. It helps to get to know your bird and its species so that, when they become ill and lose their appetite, you know what to entice them with.

Separation anxiety

Parrots are prone to forming very close bonds with their human companions if they are not kept with other parrots. Alex the galah stopped eating and started wasting away when his owner went overseas for a month. The owner's father was the unfortunate carer left to worry himself sick that Alex would no longer be around when his son returned. Multiple visits to the vet revealed no sign of illness other than lack of appetite. All sorts of plans were formulated to try to get Alex interested in eating again. Poor Alex remained miserable and only ate under extreme duress. He wouldn't sing, he wouldn't dance. All seemed lost until his owner returned. The recovery was miraculous. The owner's father had been so sure that Alex was on death's door and had been such a frequent visitor to the vet that he made his son bring Alex to the vet clinic to show us how Alex normally behaved. The all-singing, all-dancing, all-eating Alex was indeed a sight to see.

Obesity

At the other end of the scale are birds that consume a diet far too high in energy for their needs. This is often seen in caged parrots such as budgies, cockatiels, galahs and sulphur-crested cockatoos that are fed too many sunflower seeds.

Peanuts the sulphur-crested cockatoo arrived at the Lort Smith Animal Hospital with a most uncomfortable condition. She had suffered a prolapsed cloaca due to the pressure of some fatty tumours she had developed. You see, Peanuts was named for her addiction. She loved eating peanuts. Unfortunately, this addiction had been indulged far too frequently. Peanuts are very high in fat and this had led to her becoming obese. She had developed the fatty tumours which had led to her prolapse. By the time she arrived to see us she had lost her appetite and rapidly lost weight, but the tumours remained. Poor Peanuts had to go through many surgeries before she was able to keep all of her private parts tidily tucked away inside her cloaca where they belonged.

Is your bird overweight?

The body condition of birds is usually assessed by the amount of flesh over their keel. The keel is the breast plate of birds. It covers the front of the chest and is a flat plate with a sharp protrusion which runs in a line from the top of the plate to near the pelvis. It is indeed shaped like a boat's keel. You should always be able to feel this bone as a hard line or slight protrusion along the middle of your bird's chest. The flesh on either side should not obscure it completely. If it does, your bird is overweight. If, however, there is very little flesh on either side of the keel and it protrudes sharply, your bird is underweight. It is a good idea to compare your bird to others to get a feel for this method of assessing a bird's weight. Alternatively, ask your vet to assess her weight for you and measure the actual weight in grams. Once you know the weight you can monitor any weight loss or gain yourself, using kitchen scales.

A balanced diet is the key to careful weight loss in obese birds. It is important they do not lose weight too quickly or they may become ill. Change the diet gradually. Reduce the amount of sunflower seeds (nuts too if your bird gets them). Don't offer high carbohydrate treats of human food such as peanut butter sandwiches, cakes, biscuits or sweets. Encourage your bird to eat more green feed and vegetables by pretending to eat them with her. Work out a program with your vet and stick to it. At the same time, continue to monitor her food intake and weight to make sure she hasn't stopped eating altogether.

Food that birds should avoid

Avocado

Some parrots have been known to die after eating a particular type of avocado. It is safest to avoid feeding avocado products of any kind (flesh, seed or skin) to parrots.

Avocado flesh, seeds and skin should not be offered to parrots due to their toxic effects.

Affected birds sit with wings held away from the body, breathe faster than usual and sometimes vomit. Their breast muscles can swell and they can also suffer nervous system symptoms.

Caffeine

Coffee, non-herbal tea, and any food or drink containing caffeine (including chocolate) should be reserved for people. It is not bird food, even for a snack.

Match diets to species

Rainbow lorikeets are nectar-eating birds and will do very poorly on diets based on seed. They need a well-balanced nectar replacement solution.

Granivorous birds will develop diarrhoea and gastrointestinal disease when fed too much fruit.

Heavy metal poisoning

Parrots love to chew, tear, dismantle and eat things they should not. . When left to their own devices they are renowned for eating wires and undoing fixtures on cages. It is essential that you only furnish and secure cages with items that cannot be taken apart by a parrot and that do not contain lead or zinc, which are the metals responsible for causing heavy metal poisoning. The symptoms are often just a subdued parrot with salmon-pink urates. (Urates are the white part of the droppings.)

It is also very risky to leave parrots wandering unsupervised, even for a moment, around your house. You may think you have removed all dangers to your parrot but I am certain they will discover things you never knew you had: small toys, mirrors, key rings, galvanised pots, plant fertiliser, flaking paint and hair pins, just to name a few.

reptiles

what do reptiles need?

154
Meals

164
Beverages

166
Party food, treats and snacks

168
Reptiles feeling poorly

171
Food that reptiles should avoid

Reptiles are an entirely different kettle of fish when it comes to digestion of their food. We mammals produce our own heat to enable our body to function at a certain rate. Reptiles need an external source of heat to fire up their metabolism. They cannot properly digest their food in cool conditions. In the wild, this usually happens gradually and coincides with a loss of appetite and a slowing down of all body functions. When we keep lizards, turtles and snakes as pets we are responsible for providing them with the right conditions to enable them to eat and digest their food. If their heat lamp or hot rock in their enclosure stops working, or they are moved to a cooler room with poor temperature regulation, they cannot go exploring for a basking spot in the sun or a warm nest in the leaf litter under trees as they would in the wild. They just get colder and then their body cannot continue with its normal functions even if they have just eaten a meal.

The most important part of a reptile's diet is actually the environment in which it is served! The temperature must be within a specific range, the lighting must be just right, and the furnishings must be arranged to provide optimal access to both. Ultraviolet (UV) light, day length, temperature and humidity requirements are species-specific, so it is very important to know your own pet's particular needs. They are also very particular about whom they chose to eat with. Two pythons cannot eat together in case one ends up inside the other!

Snakes

Snakes are strict carnivores. They must be fed whole prey and that prey must be appropriate to the species kept. Experienced herpetologists keep a wide range of snakes: from king cobras that eat only other snakes, to mangrove snakes that hunt for birds and lizards in trees. The most common snakes kept as pets are pythons and they are comparatively easy to feed. Commercially produced rats and mice are easy to find and are supplied and fed dead, not live. Snakes get their vitamin D from their prey and do not require UV lighting to be able to use it.

Lizards

Lizards are many and varied and different species will require different diets. Some lizards are able to convert and use the vitamin D from their diet but others require UV light to do this. Without it, they will end up with soft delicate bones. The more common lizard pets I have treated are blue-tongues, bearded dragons, shinglebacks and various water dragons. They all eat insects and other whole prey but also require vegetable matter to balance their diets. Blue-tongue lizards actually like quite a bit of fruit in their diet, but will also happily eat too much very sweet fruit which will make them sick. Water dragons have caused me terrible worries as I have had to do all sorts of surgical and medical repairs of damaged faces and jaws when they jump at prey or into the water and injure themselves on the glass front of the vivaria. Injuries can also be caused by inappropriately designed enclosures with sharp or rough edges that the lizards may try to extract prey from or try to escape through. Mesh is a particular danger to reptiles.

Turtles

Australian freshwater turtles are carnivores. Long-necked turtles rely mostly on whole prey like fish, crustaceans, and even insects. Macquarie turtles will eat more plant matter but they still rely on hunting as a major part of their diet. It is essential that this diet offers all the nutrients they require and this means feeding plant and vegetable matter as well as muscle meat. A turtle that has access to a garden and a pond with duckweed on it will get some of its vitamin, fibre and mineral requirements by grazing itself. A turtle housed indoors will need much closer attention. Balanced calcium and vitamin supplements are also essential to their wellbeing. Vitamin D is needed for them to be able to use the dietary calcium. They cannot use the vitamin D from their diet unless they have access to an appropriate UV light source. Without it they end up with a condition like rickets in humans. The bones and shell go soft and become deformed. A common mistake that inexperienced turtle keepers make is not realising that UV light from the sun is ineffective when filtered by glass. Turtles housed indoors need to be taken outside for 20 minutes per day or provided with a complete artificial source of UV light.

Meals

Reptiles are very different from mammals in how often they need to eat. Many adult lizards and turtles only need to eat twice weekly. Young ones need to be fed daily. In winter they often don't eat at all. Snakes should only eat after they have defecated between meals! Small snakes need to eat more often than large ones. Large reticulated pythons (up to 5 metres long) may only eat once in 6 months in the wild.

Remember the keys to feeding reptiles: balanced diet, preferred temperature range, UV light, and appropriate frequency of feeding.

Pythons

Pythons eat infrequently and digest their food very slowly. Their intestines grow and thicken every time they eat a meal to enable digestion to take place in a tube that is merely part of the length of their body. Humans rely on several hundred metres of thin-walled intestines and plenty of heat to digest their food.

Pet pythons are fed a diet of mice and rats. The size of the mouse or rat fed will depend on the size of the python.

The interesting thing about whole prey, like rodents, is that you need to consider whether the diet of the prey is well-balanced. If it is not, then it will not provide good nutrition for your pet.

Commercially produced rats and mice may arrive well-fed and well-balanced but, if you buy them in bulk (and not already dead) and have to keep them for more than a day, you need to consider their diet. Rodent pellets are readily available commercially.

Prey

At this point I can't help but mention the occupational health-hazard that people face when caring for animals that would be hunters if left in the wild state. We need to consider that many of these animals may consider us to be potential prey items. Even if they don't remember that they are predators they have pretty good weapons — teeth, claws and great dexterity and speed — with which to defend themselves if they feel they are in danger. Reptiles are often viewed with fear but tame reptiles are really no more dangerous, possibly less so, than your average pet dog or cat. As a child I was bitten on the face by a friend's labrador retriever and the only serious bite I have suffered was when a cat bit into my knuckle. Although I have known keepers to be bitten by cobras and crocodiles, most tame reptiles are less likely to bite than your average pussy cat! A zoo colleague of mine was bitten by a wild python (he says it was his fault, and not the python's, for putting the python back in its bag carelessly) and asked me to stitch his hand for him so that we could continue working. I'm happy to say it healed with only a very fine scar. Once, when I had a tiger under anaesthesia, she stirred and tried to sit up after someone trod on her tail. She looked straight at me before lying down unconscious again. Now I know what a hunted deer feels like. Even so we all still work with the animals we love and try to find ways to convince them that we are neither a danger to them, nor dinner items!

Monty python

Pythons have very flexible mouths that allow them to swallow much bigger prey than you would expect from the size of their heads and bodies. They need to have very healthy mouths to be able to eat. Monty the python was refusing to eat the mice offered to him by his owner. He was presented to me to figure out what was going on. When we opened his mouth we found that he had broken a tooth and the gums were swollen and red around it. Monty's owner confessed that he had been offering Monty food more often because he was worried about his lack of appetite. It turned out that what Monty needed was a good rest from having to eat. Every time he tried to hold onto his food it would hurt his mouth and slow down the healing process. We gave him a couple of months off from having to try to eat and then started afresh. Now Monty is right as rain.

Seafood marinara for two

Long-necked turtles

When serving food for your turtle consider how these animals would eat in the wild. Long-necked turtles much prefer to eat in the water rather than on land and may refuse to eat if that is where their food is placed.
Here's a recipe you can both enjoy. I'll start with a little cautionary note. Reptiles carry a variety of bacteria that do not make them sick but can make us very sick indeed. Please wash your hands thoroughly before handling food if you have handled your pet turtle.
Go to the market and buy a marinara mix or create you own. Set aside ¼ cup of the mix and a teaspoon of parsley for your turtle and keep the rest for spaghetti marinara for you! Here's my favourite blend.

suitable for

turtle, dog, cat, human

preparation time

Medium: 15–45 minutes to prepare and cook.

ingredients

- ½ cup prawns (shells removed)
- ½ cup salmon fillet cubes
- ¼ cup scallops
- 1 cup tinned roma tomatoes
- ½ cup white wine
- 2 garlic cloves
- ½ cup hand-torn fresh Italian parsley
- 200 g spaghetti
- olive oil
- parmesan

method

for the turtle

Wash the seafood under tap water to reduce the salt content. Remove the heads from the prawns and peel them. Reserve a ¼ cup of mixed scallops, salmon and prawns and the raw prawn heads for your turtle. Add a teaspoon of torn parsley and mix well.

serve

Offer it fresh and raw to your turtle.

for the human

Fill a large saucepan with water and bring to the boil.
Throw in a generous pinch of salt and the pasta. Cook according to the instructions on the packet.
Finely chop or mince the garlic.
Pour some olive oil into a warm deep-sided frying pan and add the garlic.
Throw the fish in and cook over moderate heat until it loses its translucency.
Add the tomatoes and white wine.
Bring to the boil and turn off the heat.
Strain the pasta and add it to the marinara in the frying pan. Tip in the parsley. Mix well.

serve

Serve with freshly grated parmesan, black pepper and a glass of wine.

Seafood marinara for two

Dragons and skinks

In the wild, lizards such as bearded dragons, blue-tongues and shinglebacks eat a variety of invertebrates (creatures such as worms, snails and crickets), small vertebrates (baby mice and rats, other lizards) and plant matter. Wild lizards don't get access to much fruit but captive lizards will eat it like we eat chocolate. Developing a liking for something doesn't make it a healthy staple diet for them. Fruit should be fed infrequently or only in very small amounts.

As a rule, lizards under 12 months of age should be fed insects every day but don't force them to grow too fast.

Feed lizards older than 12 months no more than three times a week.

The recipe opposite should be fed in moderation. Lizards need to eat plenty of crunchy insects at each meal to prevent dental disease.

Beef terrine

suitable for

lizard, turtle, dog, cat, ferret

preparation time

Long: over 45 minutes to prepare and cook.

ingredients

500 g minced beef
3 slices bacon
2 chicken breast fillets
⅓ cup dried fruit
¼ cup unsweetened apple juice
olive oil
1 garlic clove, crushed
½ cup chopped parsley (or duckweed if you have it)
2 eggs
1 cup breadcrumbs

method

Soak the dried fruit in the apple juice for 1 hour. Drain well.
Preheat oven to 180 °C.
Finely slice, and then mince the bacon and chicken.
Beat the eggs.
Add the parsley, eggs, breadcrumbs and soaked fruit to the minced meats. Mix well.
Spoon the mixture into a loaf tin. Press down firmly. Cover with foil.
Place the tin into another baking dish and fill with hot water half way up the height of the tin.
Bake for 1 hour.
Remove from water. Place a weight on top and allow it to cool.
Refrigerate or freeze in portions.

serve

Serve at room temperature.

Skink's supper

suitable for

lizard

preparation time

Short: 5–15 minutes to prepare.

ingredients

1 teaspoon chopped apple, pear, orange or melon
1 teaspoon chopped carrot
1 teaspoon chopped broccoli or watercress
2 cm cube of meatloaf (page 6)
¼ teaspoon grated boiled egg
2 mealworms
reptile calcium supplement
reptile vitamin supplement

method

Dust mealworms with a reptile calcium supplement and a reptile vitamin supplement.
Mix together ingredients and serve.

Dragon feast

suitable for
lizard

preparation time
Short: 5–15 minutes to prepare.

ingredients
- 3 crickets
- 2 snails
- 1 teaspoon finely chopped lettuce
- 1 teaspoon finely chopped dandelion
- 1 teaspoon mashed banana
- 1 teaspoon minced beef (cooked)
- 1 quartered grape
- vitamin and mineral supplement (according to instructions on packaging)

method
This is a three-course meal for your bearded dragon. The crickets are an appetiser. The snails are the entrée. For main course, serve the ingredients separately on a tasting plate or just mix it all together. The vitamin and mineral supplement is most effectively consumed when mixed well into the minced beef.

Keeping your crickets healthy

ingredients
- peat moss
- lettuce and cabbage leaves
- sliced carrot and apple
- dry dog food

method
Place a 5–10 cm layer of peat moss on the floor.
Provide cardboard hides for crickets.
Provide wet sponges in water dishes.
Add food.
Change food and sponges daily.

Substrate for mealworms

I will describe depths and relative proportions of ingredients so that they are easy to adjust according to your storage container.

ingredients
- 1 cm depth wheat bran
- 1 cm depth dried oats
- 1 tablespoon wheat germ

method
Pop your fresh mealworms in.
Place newspaper on top.
Sprinkle the newspaper with a little water.
Place 1 tablespoon of shredded carrot, broccoli or apple on the paper.
Change vegetables daily.
Sprinkle the newspaper with water every second day.
Keep container warm at 22–30 °C. Allow them to be exposed to natural day and night hours.

A healthy food chain

It is fascinating to study and manipulate the food chain. The food that is given to an animal must be well-balanced and, in the case of carnivores, this means that their prey must be well-balanced. Pygmy possums in the Victorian Alps eat large fatty moths as an important part of their diet leading up to the breeding season. These moths come to rest in the mountains during one season of their life cycle. During their breeding season, the eggs are laid and the caterpillars hatch and feed on crops that have had over a hundred years of treatment with insecticides. Residues of these insecticides are found in the pygmy possum's droppings. The food chain is vast and it can be complex to get to the root of complications.

Commercially produced crickets, mealworms, blood worms and many others may arrive well-fed and well-balanced but, if you buy them in bulk (and not already dead) and have to keep them for more than a day, you need to consider their diet.

Adjacent are some recipes for keeping crickets and mealworms healthy and nutritionally balanced for your lizards.

Beverages

No matter what the species, pets must always be supplied with fresh clean water and it must be changed regularly. As you can see from previous chapters, there are different methods for animals to obtain water and it needs to be supplied in a form that your pet can use.

A common source of water for those animals that cannot visit waterholes are the dew drops on leaves in the morning. It is very important with some frogs and lizards in captivity to spray mist their vivarium to provide the moisture they need to hydrate themselves. Making the enclosure too damp can also be a problem and result in higher levels of disease. Pythons need a container of water big enough to soak their entire body in and heavy enough not to tip over. I have found that they are less inclined to drink from a small bowl that they can only dip their heads into, especially when they are sick.

Bearded dragon watering

Dragons should be sprayed with water on alternate days. If it is very hot and dry, they should be sprayed daily.

Turtle watering

Australian freshwater turtles are semi-aquatic, meaning they spend only part of their time out of the water. The quality and temperature of their water is very important. Not only for drinking but also for general body and shell health. They eat in the water and it is also their toilet.

Rules for maintaining water quality include:

1 Maintain your filtration system.
2 Remove any uneaten food immediately. Don't leave it in the tank until the next day. It will rot and contaminate the water.
3 Choose food that doesn't partially dissolve in the tank water and cause contamination. If the food is likely to break up, then scoop some of the tank water into a bucket and feed your turtle in there instead of in the tank.
4 Maintain water temperature at the correct range for the species of turtle that you own.

Snake watering

Pythons like to be able to submerse their entire body in water. You will need to provide a heavy-based dish big enough to accommodate your python and small enough for the python to climb out of with ease. The water should be kept clean and changed frequently.

Party food, treats and snacks

This is where you get to let loose a little. I have lectured you on the importance of keeping your lizard's teeth healthy and suggested ways of getting your turtle to eat more than just meat. But we all like to have something special every now and then so we like to pass on this joy to our pets. I love to see the enthusiastic tilt of the head and scuttling of limbs when a lizard or turtle is given something they crave. Just remember it's all about balance and you mustn't give too much.

A lizard's dessert

suitable for
lizard

preparation time
Short: 5–15 minutes to prepare.

ingredients
½ teaspoon chopped orange
½ teaspoon chopped melon
1 teaspoon chopped broccoli
1 teaspoon chopped watercress
1 pinky mouse (defrost in fridge overnight)

method
Mix ingredients together.

The dragon's teeth

suitable for
lizard

preparation time
Short: 5–15 minutes to prepare.

ingredients
2 big crunchy cockroaches
2 big crunchy crickets
1 cm cubed sweet potato
1 cm cubed carrot
1 cm cubed broccoli

method
Mix ingredients together.

Freshwater turtle treat

In their natural habitat, Australian freshwater turtles such as long-necked turtles eat molluscs, crustaceans, small mussels, tadpoles, frogs, small fish and insects.
If your turtle is fed a pelleted diet or a red meat-based diet they may appreciate some whole fish.

suitable for
turtle

preparation time
Short: 5–15 minutes to prepare.

ingredients
frozen whitebait
2 yabbies

method
Keep some whitebait frozen and give them as treats.
Feed fresh yabbies as they have the best nutritional value. No cooking is necessary. They may be fed whole or chopped into cubes. Leave the shell on.

tip
Remember to remove the uneaten pieces from the tank to prevent putrefaction.

Is my reptile the right weight?

Lizards are often assessed by the amount of fat in their tails. A very rounded tail in a water dragon, bearded dragon or iguana is likely to indicate a lizard in good condition. It is not often that I have seen pet lizards overweight. I have, however, seen large monitor lizards in captivity that have become overweight. Their tails and their entire bodies become very well-rounded indeed.

Snakes that are fed too often can become overweight. They keep their fat on the inside of their bodies which makes body condition assessment interesting. When handling snakes you become accustomed to the feel of the weight of their body compared to their size. A fat snake feels very heavy compared to his length, and when feeling along their abdomen they feel very dense. When combined with a history of feeding too often and ruling out constipation, it is likely that the snake is indeed overweight.

I have never seen a fat turtle. Turtles are sometimes presented severely bloated due to systemic disease, and nutritional disease and they are indeed heavy in that situation but it is not due to fat. More commonly I have seen very underweight turtles. Turtles often don't show many signs of illness that are visible to the untrained eye. They often hide their symptoms until they become too weak to swim properly or to beg for food. It is often at this stage that they are presented at the vet clinic.

Reptiles feeling poorly

The most common reasons for reptile patients being presented to me are related to dietary mineral imbalances, poor environmental temperature control and lack of exposure to UV light.

One of my favourite patients thus far has been the delightfully cuddly Rexy, the bearded dragon, who suffered a prolapsed cloaca. The lining of her cloaca (the single opening for urination, defecation and the passage of eggs in lizards) had everted. If it were allowed to remain outside her body her life would soon be at risk. She was rushed into emergency surgery with us and has come back to visit for aftercare on several occasions. She loves to sit on shoulders where she can absorb our warmth and watch the world with great interest and animation. What a delightful patient! We suspect that she was suffering from a lack of calcium in her diet as the owner had changed from one brand of vitamin and mineral supplement to another and hadn't realised there was no calcium in it.

We have seen several turtles with shell injuries and disease. Pathology of the shell is a very common disease among pet turtles. It is occasionally due to injuries but more often due to owners unwittingly missing an important ingredient in their pet turtle's home management. The most important part of treating our reptile patients is developing home improvement plans. This involves dietary modifications, provision of an appropriate UV light source, heat of the right kind and temperature range, control of humidity and design of cage furnishings. Sometimes a complete lifestyle change is needed. On other occasions only minor modifications need to be made.

Many pythons, lizards and turtles slow down and refuse food during winter in southern Australia. This can come as a surprise to inexperienced owners when temperature and lighting is not well-regulated for their pet. Some reptiles will slow down in winter and eat less even when their environment seems well-controlled, because their in-built body clock tells them it is winter. This slowing down of body functions is called brumation. It is a good idea not to induce brumating conditions if you are an inexperienced reptile keeper or if your pet is not in excellent body condition prior to winter. However, if your reptile pet doesn't show interest in food in winter, then don't feed him as it will do more harm than good. If you are uncertain whether a lack of appetite is due to season or disease, have your reptile examined by someone experienced rather than force-feeding him.

Malnutrition and dental disease

Bopal the blue-tongue lizard belonged to an inexperienced owner. The poor little lizard had a bloated belly and soft bones. His favourite food was papaya and he was given plenty every day. He was also offered garden grubs and vegetables but chose to eat the sweet papaya instead. The high amount of sugar in his diet was the perfect environment for disease in his intestines and made him fat and bloated. The lack of calcium meant his bones went soft and folded under his heavy body weight. Once he was fed a more balanced diet his health improved, he regained strength and he was ready to face the world as a new lizard.

One of the most common problems I've seen in pet and exhibited lizards is poor dental health, which often manifests as stomatitis or 'mouth rot'. Lizards need big, crunchy insects for dental health. Insects for a bearded dragon achieve the same results as raw bones in dogs and cats. They help keep teeth healthy and strong, both through their physical properties and their nutrient content. Salads and fruit may be a nice treat for your lizard but what they really need are crunchy staples to encourage their longevity. The insects chosen as food for the dragon must also have had a well-balanced diet and be very healthy to be able to provide what the lizard needs (see Dragon's teeth recipe page 167).

Food that reptiles should avoid

Vitamin toxicity

It's all about balance. Too much of one nutrient can result in too little of another.

If the meat that you feed to your reptile is very fatty, then the natural anti-oxidants in the diet will be depleted. Too much of one fat soluble vitamin (for instance vitamin A) can result in too little of another (such as vitamin D). Turtles have been known to suffer from a deficiency of vitamin A and then become ill from vitamin A toxicosis when over-supplemented. Too much phosphorous can upset the body's ability to use calcium. Too much dietary vitamin D can lead to hardening of the wrong tissues in the body.

Find the right supplements for your particular reptile and don't overdo it.

Feed hygeine

The quality of the food is very important. Rancid meat should not be fed to turtles or lizards. Mealworms growing on a mould-infested substrate may cause illness in the animal that eats them.

Guaranteed supplement delivery

Reptile owners often talk about 'gut-loading' and 'dusting' the insect ingredients in their pets' diets. They are referring to methods of supplying valuable vitamin and mineral supplements to their pets. Gut-loading usually involves feeding the insects a diet very dense in calcium for 24 hours prior to harvesting. Dusting refers to placing the insects in a container with the supplement and coating them in it before feeding them to the pet. Both methods are successful at delivering supplements as long as the dusted items are eaten dry and immediately. If not, the supplement tends to brush or wash off the dusted items.

rabbits and guinea pigs

what do rabbits and guinea pigs need?

176
Meals

182
Beverages

182
Party food, treats and snacks

185
Rabbits and guinea pigs feeling poorly

188
Food that rabbits and guinea pigs should avoid

It all starts with grass.

It is fascinating to find out what makes a creature tick. Becoming a vet allowed me to start discovering some of what lay beneath. My first job was in a country town in a dairying community. Our work involved the medical care of dairy and beef cows, deer, ostriches and cats and dogs. We would also take it in turns to do the meat inspection for the local abattoir. The science of growing grass and feeding it to cows, goats and sheep is quite astonishing, but I promise you I won't take you through it. This is where I started to see the importance of every ingredient that enters the body. Every ingredient eaten is a building block and the end-product cannot be complete without all the right tools and ingredients. The science of that was obvious but the art of it became clearer over the years that I worked in different countries and with all sorts of veterinary practices from cats and dogs on the surf beaches of Sydney to zoo animals in Asia.

Rabbits and guinea pigs are herbivores. This means they eat a plant-based diet, but this is where the similarity ends. The range of herbivores is vast, from cows and giraffes to manatees and dugongs that live in the sea, so it is really not a very useful definition when trying to feed your pet.

Rabbits have a most interesting digestive system. They rely heavily on little organisms that colonise their caecum, which is part of the intestines. We have an appendix, which is the human equivalent, but we barely use ours and it is tiny. The caecum in the rabbit is one of the most important parts of its digestive system. The bugs that grow inside it actually digest the fibre part of the diet for the rabbit. The rabbit can then use the products from this to fuel all its functions. Interestingly enough, horses and hippos also do this to digest their high-fibre diet. Unlike most other herbivores, rabbits and guinea pigs are coprophagic. This means that they produce special faecal pellets that they eat. These are often called night pellets. Rabbits and guinea pigs obtain many of their vitamin requirements from these pellets, which also help to maintain the right balance of organisms living inside the caecum.

Grass. It is very interesting to watch it grow despite rumours to the contrary! High-quality, fast-growing lush pasture of particular kinds can be a decadent feast in a cow's eyes. It can also kill them because of the imbalance of nutrients in it. Too much of a good thing can be dangerous for any species and they don't necessarily know to stop themselves. Consider this when offering your rabbit lush watery lettuce, a whole apple or some bread. Stop, think, and then look at the safe treat section in this chapter for some new ideas.

Meals

Rabbits need to eat a high-fibre, grass-based diet. Good quality grass hay and a little fresh green pick (fresh grass, clover, dandelions and dark green leafy vegetables) are all they need. Lucerne hay and pellets are useful for young growing rabbits, but the high calcium content can cause urinary tract problems in adult rabbits.

Guinea pigs, unlike rabbits, are actually rodents but they are herbivores, not omnivores. Their diet should be high fibre (grass hay is good) with fresh vegetables and a little fruit and grain. The vegetables are important to guinea pigs as they cannot make their own vitamin C. They need a source in their diet, just like us.

Fibre digesting techniques

It is so important to know what sort of food is appropriate for a particular species and what it can and cannot digest. You need to know what goes on inside the animal as well as the long-term effects of malnutrition from the outside. The range of digestive systems in animals is vast. Cows, manatees (also known as sea cows) and proboscis monkeys have a complex stomach that uses bacteria and other tiny organisms to help digest the fibre in their food. It's called fermentative digestion. Rabbits, hippos and elephants use their caecum to digest their fibre in a similar manner. When looking after the diets of these animals it is important to also look after their bacteria or else the bad guys will take over and all hell will break loose.

This is all very well, I hear you say, but what should I feed my rabbit? A high-fibre diet is the answer. They are actually so efficient at digesting coarse roughage that they are better off being fed ordinary grass hay and straw rather than something high-protein like lucerne or clover. Just like any other animal, they also need their own unique balance of nutrients including vitamins and minerals.

Fresh greens and hay

suitable for
rabbit, bird, guinea pig, rodent

preparation time
Short: 5–15 minutes to prepare.

ingredients
- 500 g grass hay
- 1 cup freshly cut grass
- ¼ cup freshly picked clover
- 4 green beans
- 2 celery tops (the leaves from the top of a stick of celery)
- 6 carrot tops (just the leaves from freshly picked carrots)
- ½ cm slice of carrot (no more!)

serving method
Rinse your ingredients with clean water and serve immediately.

tip
Alternative greens include dandelions and radish tops.

Guinea pig salad

Pelleted diets designed for guinea pigs will have added ascorbic acid to meet their vitamin C requirements.

If you are feeding a whole-food diet to your guinea pig you will either need to add ascorbic acid to the drinking water or ensure he is fed plenty of vitamin C-rich vegetables and leafy greens.

suitable for

guinea pig, rodent

preparation time

Short: 5–15 minutes to prepare.

ingredients

1 cup fresh dandelion greens
¼ peeled orange
¼ tomato
1 brussels sprout
1 broccoli floret
1 strawberry

serving method

Chop and mix ingredients together.

Sprouts for guinea pigs

Consider sprouting some of the following to supplement your guinea pig's diet.

suitable for

guinea pig, rodent

preparation time

Long: over 45 minutes to prepare.

ingredients

fenugreek
alfalfa
snow peas
wheat
barley

method

The key to sprouting is fresh clean seeds and warm but not-too-moist conditions. See the Bird chapter for ideas on how to sprout seeds (page 132).

serve

Rinse sprouts under cold water and serve by the handful.

Beverages

Rabbits and guinea pigs will happily drink from either a bowl or a bottle with a nozzle. The water must always be clean. This means washing the bottle with detergent and changing the water daily, especially during warmer weather.

Animals eating a high-moisture diet such as fresh grass and vegetables will not need to drink as much. However, animals fed mainly hay or chaff, pellet and grain mixes will need to drink plenty.

Party food, treats and snacks

Rabbits and guinea pigs need to eat lots of hay and not very much in the way of starchy vegetables or sugary fruit. They may love apples and lettuce but these are far too easily fermented in the caecum and can cause diarrhoea, bloat and even stop the gut working.

A couple of thin slices of apple are ok but hay and dark green leafy vegetables and herbs are the best.

Assessment of rabbit body condition

Rabbits have heavy hind quarters and very delicate forequarters by design and this can make their weight difficult to assess. Use your hands. As with the other mammals, in a rabbit in good body condition that is not obese, you should be able to feel ribs and the points of the hips. Sharply protruding hips indicate an underweight rabbit. Barely palpable hips usually indicate a fat rabbit. The size of the abdomen is not a good guide as an enlarged or bloated abdomen often indicates illness rather than obesity.

Guinea pig's vitamin C

A dietary source of vitamin C is needed by guinea pigs. One way of providing the vitamin C is in their drinking water.

ingredients

1000 mg ascorbic acid
500 ml water

method

Dissolve the ascorbic acid in the drinking water and add to the guinea pigs' water bottle daily.

Treats for rabbits

suitable for

rabbit, rodent

preparation time

Short: 5–15 minutes to prepare.

ingredients

1 slice of apple, 0.5 cm thick
2–3 raisins
1 pistachio nut
pinch of oatmeal
apple cider
dish of herbal tea

serve

Serve treats fresh to your rabbit.

Tunnelling

Guinea pigs love to burrow and create tunnels. Give them a big pile of loosened grass hay or straw and they will spend hours creating their own maze in it. They can also eat it and it will be good for them.

Rabbits and guinea pigs feeling poorly

Rabbits are mostly fastidious groomers and hairballs can be a problem especially in those with long hair. A long-haired cat can regurgitate hair, but it is physically impossible for a rabbit to vomit. Both can benefit from dietary assistance with this condition. The signs in a rabbit aren't as clear as in cats because rabbits cannot regurgitate hairballs. The rabbit often just stops eating as much and produces fewer faecal pellets. If your rabbit loses its appetite or suffers a sudden reduction in faecal output she should be taken to the vet to rule out the more sinister causes.

Rabbits don't respond well to pastes and certainly can't eat cat food designed to reduce hair shedding, so what do you do? Rabbits need a high-fibre diet. Feeding them plenty of grass hay and allowing daily access to fresh grass will help reduce the build up of hair.

Good diet, in combination with brushing them daily will help reduce the occurrence of gastric fur balls.

Many owners feed lucerne hay or pellet-based diets to their rabbits. These diets are too high in energy for the average pet rabbit. This results in fat rabbits. Lucerne is also high in calcium. High calcium diets can cause the formation of thick creamy urine and can contribute to urinary tract and kidney disease.

Learning from Flossy's mistakes

Poor little Flossy the dwarf-lop rabbit had a habit of chewing on the skirting boards and the plaster. After a while, the plaster started to make concretions in her intestines and the food would no longer move along, no matter how hard those little intestines tried. Flossy stopped passing any solid faeces and then stopped eating. For a while it seemed as if she had diarrhoea because that was all that could get around the solid blockage in her intestines. Eventually, even that stopped. But Flossy was a tough rabbit. She had to go to surgery to have the blockage removed, and after a week in hospital and some careful home care, she recovered.

Rabbits are renowned for chewing and even eating inappropriate things, especially when kept as indoor pets. They will gnaw on electrical cords, munch away at skirting boards, nibble carpets, redesign table legs and even eat plasterboard. There are several problems with allowing this to occur. The least important is that it damages your house and furnishings. The most important is that it is potentially harmful and even lethal to your rabbit. Consider the potential for electrocution when electrical cords are damaged. The paint in old houses often contains lead and this can poison your rabbit if she chews on it. Even plasterboard is dangerous when consumed frequently.

High-fibre diet for rabbits

This is an excellent diet to help a rabbit recover from diarrhoea due to feeding too many easily digestible foods such as lettuce, fresh and dried fruit or even too many grains and pellets.

suitable for

rabbit

preparation time

Short: 5–15 minutes to prepare.

ingredients

- 2 kg grass hay
- 1 cup freshly picked grass and clover

serve

Serve fresh to your rabbit.

Teeth grinders

Untreated wood and branches make excellent chew toys for your rabbits and guinea pigs and provide a safe distraction for nibblers like Flossy.

suitable for

guinea pig, rodent

preparation time

Medium: 15–45 minutes to prepare.

ingredients

- cherry tree twigs
- apple tree cuttings
- plum tree branches

method

Chose branches or cuttings that are about 2–3 cm thick. Offer them to your rabbits and guinea pigs as chew toys.

Food that rabbits and guinea pigs should avoid

Brassicaceous vegetables

Vegetables such as broccoli, cabbage and kale can cause too much gas to be produced if fed in large amounts to rabbits and guinea pigs.

High-oxalate vegetables

Green such as spinach, beet leaves and to a lesser extent parsley can have high levels of oxalates. Fed in high amounts these can interfere with calcium metabolism and cause damage to kidneys. Carnivores are unlikely to consume enough of these to cause a problem but herbivores such as rabbits and guinea pigs could be at risk if fed these greens as the bulk of their diet. They are not a problem if fed in small amounts to healthy animals.

Grain-based diets

These are too high in energy and do not contain enough effective roughage. The high energy results in fat pets and the lack of roughage contributes to dental disease and poor intestinal health.

rodents

what do rodents need?

192
Meals

192
Beverages

195
Party food, treats and snacks

196
Rodents feeling poorly

198
Food that rodents should avoid

There are 30 families of rodents. They include animals as different as the South American capybara and the brush-tailed porcupine. However, the rodents we will talk about here are rats and mice. Rats and mice are omnivorous. They can survive on a wide variety of ingredients and are renowned for being successful scavengers. When they are offered a wide range of ingredients, they will choose their favourites rather than a balanced range of what is good for them. Well-formulated balanced pelleted diets are easily available for rats and mice, and feeding these solves the problem of rodents choosing the wrong types of food for themselves. They should also be fed a variety of vegetables, especially the green leafy types. Rats and mice are curious and they like to investigate new things. Introduce them to ingredients other than pellets when they are young and they will always be keen to try something new.

Meals

Rodents will usually enjoy vegetables either cooked or raw. Preparing a meal for a rat or mouse can be as easy as keeping aside a little of each of the ingredients that you eat at each meal.

Beverages

Fresh water must be available at all times. Rodents may obtain some of the moisture they need from their diet but they still need to drink. This is especially important if they are fed a pelleted diet. Mice are particularly sensitive to dehydration. They must never be left without drinking water. Their water dispensing bottles must be filled every day. Provide a water bottle with a nozzle in rat and mice enclosures and remember to offer them plenty of opportunities to drink if they spend the day out and about with you.

Meals

Breakfast

suitable for
rodent

preparation time
Short: 5–15 minutes to prepare.

ingredients
- 1 fine slice apple with skin on
- 1 cm piece celery
- 1 fine slice carrot
- 1 green bean
- 1 teaspoon dry oatmeal

serving method
Mix ingredients together and serve.

Lunch

suitable for
rodent

preparation time
Short: 5–15 minutes to prepare.

ingredients
- ¼ cup fresh clover
- 2 snow peas
- 1 cm slice capsicum
- ¼ piece wholemeal bread
- ¼ teaspoon natural yoghurt

serving method
Mix ingredients together and serve.

Dinner

suitable for
rodent

preparation time
Short: 5–15 minutes to prepare.

ingredients
- 1 teaspoon muesli cereal mix (not roasted)
- 1 broccoli floret
- 1 cauliflower floret
- 1 brussels sprout
- 1 cm cube cheese

serving method
Mix ingredients together and serve.

Beverages

Frozen treats

Make drinking more interesting for your rat or mouse. Try these frozen drinks on hot summer days.

suitable for
rodent

preparation time
Long: over 45 minutes to prepare.

ingredients
- ¼ cup natural yoghurt
- 1 tablespoon fresh or frozen blueberries
- orange or apple juice

method
Blend ingredients together.
Use ice-cube trays to freeze the mixes but only put a little in the bottom of each. A large ice cube is not nearly as appetising to a small rodent as a small one.

serve
Offer these treats frozen.

Party food, treats and snacks

Rose petal salad

suitable for
rodent

preparation time
Short: 5–15 minutes to prepare.

ingredients
1 freshly picked rose
2 freshly picked nasturtiums
4 mint leaves
10 pine nuts

serving method
Make sure that no insecticides or herbicides have been used on or near the flowers.
Pluck the petals from the flowers.
Rinse all the leaves together. Shake dry.
Add the pine nuts and gently mix.

Dried fruit and barley

suitable for
rodent, bird, guinea pig

preparation time
Short: 5–15 minutes to prepare.

ingredients
1 dried apricot
1 dried apple
3 sultanas
1 teaspoon barley

serving method
Slice the apple and the apricot.
Mix all the ingredients together.
Offer a little at a time.

tip
This is an easy mix to take out if your rat accompanies you.

Rose petal sweets

This is absolutely only for very special occasions as it has sugar in it!

suitable for
rodent, ferret, bird, human

preparation time
Short: 5–15 minutes to prepare and cook.

ingredients
1 yellow rose
1 red rose
1 egg white
1 teaspoon sugar

method
Preheat oven to 150 °C.
Remove the petals from the roses and wash under running water. Lay them out on paper towel to dry.
Beat the egg white.
Brush each petal with egg white.
Sprinkle a little sugar over each.
Bake for 8–10 minutes or until crisp but not discoloured.

serve
Serve when cool.
Offer your pet no more than 2 petals per day.

Rodents feeling poorly

Rats often suffer from respiratory infections. Both rats and mice are prone to developing tumours and may need surgery to treat them. When rodents are feeling poorly they often stop eating and drinking. The resulting dehydration and lack of energy makes them feel even worse. It is very important to keep your pet's spirits up when recovering from illness or surgery. Encouraging them to drink small amounts frequently can make them feel much better surprisingly quickly.

Offer some lukewarm vegetable stock or cool honeyed mint tea.

Honeyed mint tea

suitable for
rodent, human

preparation time
Short: 5–15 minutes to prepare.

ingredients
- 10 freshly picked mint leaves
- ¼ teaspoon honey
- 1 cup boiled water

method
Rinse the mint leaves and put them in a cup. Pour boiling water over them.
Stir in the honey.
Allow the tea to steep for 5 minutes.
Strain and remove the leaves.

serve
Allow the tea to cool and serve in their water container.

Sweet vegetable consommé

suitable for
rodent, human

preparation time
Medium: 15–45 minutes to prepare and cook.

ingredients
- ¼ cup sliced sweet potato
- ¼ cup sliced carrot
- ¼ cup green beans
- 4 cups water

method
Put all the vegetables and the water into a saucepan over high heat. Bring to the boil.
Reduce heat. Simmer for 20 minutes.
Strain and remove the solids. Reserve the broth.

serve
Allow to cool and serve in a bowl.

Food that rodents should avoid

Take care when allowing your rat to roam around with limited supervision. Their natural curiosity and desire to nibble will often get them into trouble. Rose the hooded rat was allowed to ride in her owner's handbag almost everywhere she went. Rose loved it. It didn't matter what was happening in the outside world because she felt safe and comfortable among her owner's possessions and there was also plenty to play with. There was a little plastic container of nuts and dried fruit, tissues and dockets to nibble and tear, make-up to sniff, car keys to jingle, and lastly, some blister packs of her owner's tablets. Rose was fascinated by the foil and plastic of the blister packs and had plenty of time to chew her way through to explore the contents. When her owner realised what had happened she got a terrible fright. She thought that Rose had eaten some of the tablets and was afraid that she would be poisoned. Luckily it turned out that Rose had only gnawed through the plastic and had not chewed the tablets themselves. No harm was done but it was a good reminder to be cautious about what Rose was exposed to when unsupervised.

Raw Kidney Beans

These are highly toxic to rats. Do not feed raw kidney beans to rats or mice in any quantity. Other types of beans may also be toxic when fed raw or dried. It is best to only feed very well cooked beans and in tiny amounts. Remember that they only have tiny stomachs.

Glossary

Adrenal gland: An endocrine gland located at the end of each kidney. Its function includes increasing blood glucose, balancing tissue salts and producing androgens.

Anaemia: A reduction in the number of red blood cells or in the concentration of haemoglobin. The animal becomes pale and week.

Anthropomorphism: Describing animal characteristics or behaviour using terms more appropriate for humans.

Arrhythmia: An abnormal heart beat rhythm.

Avian: Relating to or resembling a bird.

Brassicaceous vegetables: Cabbage, turnip, mustard, canola leaves.

Cardiac: Of or relating to the heart.

Carnivore: An animal that feeds primarily on animal flesh.

Cloaca: A cavity into which the intestinal, urinary and genital tracts empty. A single opening at the base of the tail of a bird or reptile.

Crop: A sac-like structure in a bird in which food is briefly stored after passing down the oesophagus.

Felid: A member of the cat family. Includes domestic cats and wild big and small cats. e.g. lion, tiger, cheetah, caracal, lynx.

Folivore: An animal that depends on leaves as a major part of its diet.

Frugivore: An animal that depends on fruit as a major part of its diet.

Gizzard: The muscular stomach of birds in which hard food is broken up.

Granivore: An animal that depends on grain as a major part of its diet.

Hepatic: From or pertaining to the liver.

Herbivore: An animal that feeds entirely on plants and plant parts.

Herpetology: The study of reptiles and amphibians.

Inflammation: Condition in which part of the body becomes hot, red, swells and is painful.

Insectivore: An animal that depends on insects as a major part of its diet.

Insulin: A hormone secreted by the pancreas that controls the level of glucose in the blood.

Keel: The plate of a bird's sternum that protrudes at right angles from the chest and divides the breast muscles.

Kit: A baby ferret.

Lipidosis: A disorder of fat and oil (lipids) metabolism that results in the accumulation of lipids in tissues.

Nectarivore: An animal that depends on nectar as a major part of its diet.

Oesophagus: The tube connecting the mouth with the stomach.

Omnivore: An animal that eats any kind of food, plant or animal, indiscriminately.

Pancreas: A glandular organ located near the stomach that secretes digestive juices and insulin.

Pancreatitis: Inflammation of the pancreas.

Piscivore: An animal that depends on fish as a major part of its diet.

Prescription diet: Food scientifically formulated and commercially produced to meet the needs of animals with specific diseases.

Prolapse: The sinking or falling down of an organ or part.

Pulses: The edible seeds of plants such as peas, beans and lentils.

Regurgitate: A reverse flow of food out of the oesophagus.

Stomatitis: Inflammation of the mouth.

Strict carnivore: An animal that needs to obtain some of its nutrients from animal sources.

Urates: The white part of bird droppings. Urates are excreted by the kidneys in birds and reptiles.

Vertebrate: Any animal that has a bony skeleton and a well-developed brain.

Viscera: Internal organs of the chest and abdomen.

Vivarium: A cage used to keep animals.

Index

anchovy oil 98
apple bobbing 50
Australian grass seeds 141
avocado 149

bacon
  polenta 38
  and quail egg salad 119
beef
  aspic 116
  cakes 34
  casserole 13
  chicken and vegetables 112
  and lamb stock 28
  meatballs 64
  and pork bolognese 22
  risotto with vegetables 18
  and spinach stir-fry 18
  tartare 78
  terrine 160
Beef's Christmas dinner 91
Bee's moulded fish terrine 92
Bee's moulded pork terrine 92
biscuits, bacon and cheese 40
biscuits, oatmeal and broccoli 138
Bobby's salad 132
bone cruncher 22
brassicaceous vegetables 188
breakfast for rodents 194
bush tucker for Australian native birds 141

caffeine 149
canine couscous 20
carnivore gravy 35
casserole of roasted duck 112
cat pâté 98
cheese muffins 44
chicken
  with anchovy and parmesan cream 85
  and date muffins 46
  polpettini 65
  roasted with sautéed vegetables 8
  stock and chicken soup 59
  tagine 22
chilli soy kangaroo 20
chocolate 70, 106, 124
cooked bones 71
corn cobs 71
crickets, keeping them healthy 161

dental surgery recovery diet 123
diabetic dogs 8
dinner for rodents 194
dragon feast 161
dragon's teeth 167
dried fruit and barley 195
dried heart treats 40
dried liver treats 96
dry food
  meatballs for cats 101
  meatballs for dogs 54

duck
  casserole of roasted duck 112
  and grape agar-agar 116
  rice 85
  soup 122

fish
  agar cubes 96
  aromatherapy 102
  nuggets 84
  seafood marinara for two 158
  stock 89
fresh greens and hay 178
frozen treats for rodents 194
fruit muffins 44
fruit salad 34

green salad 133
  for ducks 133
  for parrots 133
guinea pig salad 180

hay
  fresh greens and hay 178
  high fibre diet for rabbits 186
heart, dried treats 40
heavy metal poisoning 149
hedgehog, liver 42
herbal tea 136
herbs
  scented oil 144
  tussie mussie 144

high fibre diet for rabbits 186
high-oxalate vegetables 188
honeyed mint tea 197

jelly, mint tea jelly 122

lassi 89
leaves
- bush tucker for Australian native birds 141
- vase of fresh leaves 141

lentil pasties 18
liver
- brownies 116
- dried treats 96
- hedgehog 42
- support tonic 54

lizard's dessert 167
lunch for rodents 194

marinara, seafood 158
Mate's picnic 91
Mate's raw food dinner 78
mealworms substrate 161
meatballs, chicken polpettini 65
meatballs, dry food 65, 101
meatloaf 6
meat stock 28
medication 64
milk 89
milk, the myth of 89
mince and rice 55
mint tea jelly 122
mixed seed platter 130
muffins, vegetable 44
mushrooms 71, 106

natural seed bells 138
nuggets, salmon 84

oatmeal broccoli biscuits 138
offal 42
onions 70, 106, 124
osso bucco 14

pancakes 46
pork and pear stir-fry 12
pork rubbings 35
potato, mashed 13

ravioli, pussy cat 80
restricted protein
- arancini 55
- treats for cats 101

rice
- banana and rice arancini 38
- beef risotto with vegetables 18
- mince and rice 55

Rita's birthday cake for dogs 31
roast chicken and sautéed vegetables 8
rose petal
- salad 195
- sweets 195

rosemary scented oil 144

salad
- green 133
- green salad for parrots 133
- guinea pig 180
- rose petal 195
- sprouted seed 132

salmon
- Beef's Christmas dinner 91
- nuggets 84

scent trail 50
seafood marinara for two 158
seed sticks 138
seeds
- Australian grasses 141
- mixed seed platter 130
- natural seed bells 138

shepherd's pie 13
Skink's supper 160
slow roasted vegetable and beef risotto 18
soup
- chicken 28
- sweet vegetable consommé 197

sprouted seed salad 132
sprouts for guinea pigs 180
steamed vegetables 34,130
substrate for mealworms 161
sweet roasted vegetables 36
sweet vegetable consommé 197
sweets, rose petal 195

tea
- herbal 136
- honeyed mint 197

teeth grinders 186
tonic, liver support 54
treats
- for cats on restricted protein diets 101
- for freshwater turtles 167
- for rabbits 184

Tussie mussie 144
vase of fresh leaves 141
vegetable muffins 44
vegetables
- the dragon's teeth 167
- high-oxalate 188
- raw 36
- steamed 34, 130
- sweet roasted 36
- sweet vegetable consommé 197

visceral appetiser 94
vitamin C for guinea pigs 184
weight loss, dogs 68

yoghurt
- frozen treats for rodents 194
- -iced birthday cake 31
- icy poles 119
- lassi 89

OTHER BOOKS PUBLISHED IN SUPPORT OF THE LORT SMITH ANIMAL HOSPITAL

Paws for Thought — Animal Wisdom for your day, by Bev Aisbett

Everyone who had ever had a pet, worked with animals or simply observed them closely can tell you: animals have a way of adding humour, sentiment or insight to our lives.

In *Paws for Thought*, Melbourne cartoonist Bev Aisbett has drawn from her experience of this to present dozens of examples where animals provide understanding or a new perspective in our everyday concerns.

Paws for Thought will delight and inform your day, now and for many days to come.

"At last, a book that shows our vital role in the lives of the two-legged ones." – Tom, old cat in the back lane

"Bev seems to be able to capture exactly what we've been telling humans for centuries. Well done, girl. I'll rescue you anytime." – Vivienne, St. Bernard, Brunswick

"Like, how cool is this? Recognition long overdue." – Gerry, blue-tongued lizard, Melbourne

"Hate to say it, but I told you so." – Dorothy, budgie in Mudgee

"Sheer poetry." – Anon, white guinea pig, inner suburbs

The Midnight Club children's book, by Jim Howes, beautifully illustrated by Elise Hurst.

On certain nights, when the hands on the big old clock in the animal hospital approach midnight, something changes. As the clock strikes out the twelve chimes, each and every animal in every cage, in every ward is ready.

When the last chime echoes through the dark hallways all the animals sit up. The building seems to hold its breath. Then all the locks on the cages click and the doors swing open. Without a sound, the animals gather outside for the meeting of The Midnight Club. None of them knows who will be tonight's storyteller. They only know that the stories they share are important. They have to be told…